DARE TO LIVE

The following have collaborated
in the preparation of this book

Maria-Luisa Algini (Italy)

Klaus Beurle (Germany)

Nestor and Olga Busso (Argentina)

Geneva Butz (U.S.A.)

Angelina Camps (Spain)

Sabine Laplane (France)

Isidore and Eugénie Ndaywell (Zaïre)

Joseph Ndundu (Zaïre)

Moïz Rasiwala (India)

Taizé 1974

PREPARING FOR THE WORLD-WIDE
COUNCIL OF YOUTH

Dare to Live

A CROSSROAD BOOK
THE SEABURY PRESS • NEW YORK

First published in French 1973
with the title 'Audacieuse aventure'
by Les Presses de Taizé
71460 Taizé-Communauté, France

First published in English 1973
by SPCK
Holy Trinity Church
Marylebone Road
London NW1 4DU

The Seabury Press
815 Second Avenue
New York, N.Y. 10017

© Les Presses de Taizé, 1973
ISBN: 0-8164-2582-5
Printed in the United States of America.

BV
4532
.A913
1974

FOREWORD

Those who have had anything to do with Taizé and the Council of Youth in the last two or three years have encountered freshness, hope, and a contagious lightheartedness. "The Risen Christ comes to quicken a festival in the innermost heart of man," the 1970 Easter message said, and the festive note is evident in this book. The buoyancy of spirit is not the result of an escape from the world into piety. It is rather the mirth and well-being that rise among people of goodwill who accept themselves and their role in life, and who take risks in order to love the world, their neighbor, and the Lord.

The role accepted by these thousands of young people from Africa, Asia, South America, the Pacific Ocean areas, Europe, and North America is simple but audacious. They have chosen to live the simplicity of the Gospel and to be (with no offense intended) "a sign of contradiction" to the evil ways in which men treat each other and to the acquisitive values that divide "haves" from "have nots." Like the first Franciscans, they are God's troubadours, and reactions to them are similar to those encountered by St. Francis. For some who read this book or who meet the people it describes, the encounter will be a breath of pure air. For others it may be threatening or frustrating.

Neither Taizé nor the Council of Youth promotes an ideology, a scheme, or a system. If the reader wants theological "pegs" on which to hang the Council's style, he will find hints in Jacques Ellul's thesis that a Christian is one who lives the Second Coming of Christ now, judging the world (not intentionally) by a style which takes a coming reality more seriously than the "reality" by which he is surrounded. Certainly it is a kind of Christian existentialism to dare to live by living rather than by rationalizing. The French existentialist words "disponibilité" and "engagement," describe the Council style. The words mean something like "instant availability" and "commitment." Taizé's own style as interpreted by its resident theologians also influences the Council. The titles of the books of the prior of Taizé stress the living of God's today and the dynamics of an *ad hoc* or a provisional approach to life.

But I am falling into the trap that the Council avoids. Read the book and enjoy the lightness and love, the hope and sparkle, that in no way minimize the place of tears, conflict, suffering, and death in the reconciliation which the writers are trying to undertake. Share the vision: It will not be hard if you allow the spirit that most of us limit to Christmas to move you through the account of these year-round and worldwide situations and responses.

In one of the meditations Brother Roger advises the youth to stress the Council and its motivation rather than Taizé, the place and community. He is right to do so: The idolatry of absolutizing a place or an experience is always likely and always deadly. Still, it may help the North American reader who does not know Taizé to visualize the setting and to try to feel the climate of the place. The community lives in a mini-village served by one tertiary road, branching from a secondary two-lane road, which in turn derives from a national highway many miles away. When thousands of people and hundreds of vehicles converge on Taizé, the village road becomes entirely inadequate, but the prevailing goodwill and humor have nevertheless produced the nickname "Boulevard of the Reconciliation." Commitment to the provisional, to making-do, led the brothers to knock out sections of their church's west wall and to cover the square before the church with a multi-colored circus tent during Easter meetings, in order to include under one roof, more or less, the thousands who came. That opened wall and covering tent have become an appealing sign to many of us that the Church as fortress and the Church as pilgrim people are no longer clashing concepts. In a time of transition they can mutually serve the needs of the people of God. And how visible his people become as the reconciled of many races and tongues pitch their tents, mingle their voices, and share simple meals. "The century of the common man" was a postwar slogan in the forties. Perhaps the Council gatherings are a kind of sacrament of the vision behind the slogan.

"Audacious Adventure" is the French title of this book. I like it because it sounds more like the celebration or festival that animates the Council than a moral challenge. The boldness of the writers and of their adventures is caught by an invitation to join in the dance; the dance of those who are bold to say at the same time: "Our Father," and, "our brother."

THE RT. REV. SAMUEL J. WYLIE
Bishop of Northern Michigan

CONTENTS

An open-ended book

THIS IS
AN OPEN-ENDED BOOK

We are preparing for a Council of Youth :
neither a movement, nor an institution,
but a time of preparation
where the changes of today
are the seeds of those of tomorrow.

The aim of this book is to be a means
of living together,
of feeling ourselves linked together,
even with those we do not yet know,
but who are companions
on this way of exploration.

It has questions to ask of all of us :
in all that you read here,
what strikes YOU most?
what do YOU find that corresponds
to what YOU are living?
what could you share with others?

The most important things in our lives—
prayer, the giving of self,
the struggle for justice—
go beyond mere words.

Here is a book that is attempting only
to bring to light some fragments
of a whole underground life,
attempting to give expression
to what lies at the heart
of the hopes and longings of so many of us.

3

It is impossible for all of us
preparing for the Council of Youth,
in the most diverse corners of the world,
to record here all that we are living.
The experiences of just a few people
have been taken from among countless others.

As far as you can,
do not stay on the outside,
as a spectator or a reader :
it is not enough merely to read this book through.

Our aim is to awaken
your capacity for fantasy,
and, in your thirst for liberation,
to stimulate you in a creation
which you could offer to everyone,
to invite you to express and to share
the treasures you bear within you.

Our aim is to convey something
of the thirst for prayer of a great many people,
and to let you discover
that far greater things exist
than ever we dared to hope.

If all this appeals to you,
let us begin the journey together.
There is no telling what we shall live,
what gift, what generosity we shall discover.

What are we searching for?

No two people are ever the same. Each of us is different: in temparament, nationality, politics, in our beliefs. Yet each one of us is looking for something.

What about you? What are you after? What are you searching for? For your own life, for other people, for Christ for the Church. . . ?

What kinds of questions spring to mind as you look around you at home . . . in your city . . . in your country?

And what does the word 'hope' mean to you? What are you hoping for? What is your hope based on?

The people who express themselves in the following pages are trying to give names to a whole lot of unformulated aspirations and yearnings; yet not one of them is speaking in place of you; for nobody can do that.

What are you searching for?

TO FORM ONE BODY

Pierino lives in Milan, Italy, with his wife and son

There are about 4000 people living in the houses I can see from my window, houses built very close together. We live side by side and on top of one another, but we do not know each other at all. Just being neighbours is not enough to form one united body.

Every morning, we leave home, crammed together. Every evening, we come back, crammed together. Everybody crushed against each other, in the train, in the subway, or isolated in cars. But moving along together in the rush hour is not enough to form one body.

We laugh and we cry and we use what strength we have left to away from it all every time we get the chance. However, escaping together is not enough to form one body.

Our lives are rushed; we are imprisoned in factories and offices for the good of production. But there again, it is not enough to suffer together to form one body.

We are dying like flies; the air, water, and food have been poisoned; whole nations are being wiped out by war. Even dying together is not enough to form one body.

We could go on and on, giving examples like these, although it is clear that the physical conditions for forming one single body of men do exist. The technical knowledge at our disposal could favour and bring to perfection this vocation that is common to all of us; namely, to be brothers.

So is it quite vain to hope that some day men will be one? I really believe not, for the answer is already there. It can be seen in the political struggle of those who until now have had to submit.

Political involvement means building something together. In this building, each one is losing his life and thus growing in awareness, coming to accept the refining of self. If you are involved in the struggle, you will understand what I mean.

As a trade-unionist, I have seen so many workers become involved in the common struggle, just because there was no other way open, because they had been swept up in the general movement. Only later, little by little, their awareness has grown to the point where they too have become animators in the struggle and search for unity. When the objectives became common, it was no longer a question of prevailing against each other, but on the contrary, success depended on bringing together everyone's availability and creativity.

Some have dropped out on the way. But there, where many have stopped, is the starting point for others to take over and push on farther. It is a living experience. Those who were involved the most, giving themselves in their commitment for their fellow workers and for the movement in general, have grown in political maturity, and they have become more human. Their personalities were not diminished. On the contrary, they have become more complex, more rich.

Then there are comrades who kept the workers struggle alive through the most difficult times in the past, sometimes silently, often through suffering. Yet today many of them are unable to understand the changes toward the collective ideal that are taking place. But although they have got stuck on old-fashioned ideas, what they gave is right there, at the heart of the new. It is the fertile ground out of which the new has sprung up.

Such then, is my vision of the prophecy of resurrection. It is so vitally true that words and promises are insufficient. It is becoming reality. Its signification makes the word 'politics' burst apart . . .

> First the struggle, the dying,
> then, the resurrection.

For us, today, how can we actualize that new life that has been present and hidden in the Church, down through the centuries?

How can all the peoples have part in this new life?

The message of the first Christians was one of radical transformation. In what kind of world are we in turn being

9

asked to be 'first Christians'?

How can we make the Church poor, in every sense of the word? We are being asked to take the risk of hoping and of acting.

A CHURCH WHERE
EVERY MAN CAN FIND
COMMUNION

Moïz

I am from India. I remain shaken by the contact here with
a hard social reality, the raging materialistic attitudes, the
petty political games, the search for power, and the use made
of it. I am sure that our Indian spirituality is still there, but
where can it be found? I have just been to the north of the
country, to Delhi and in the Rajastan. Crossing the Rajastan,
I saw scenes of senseless cruelty. A girl of ten was crying
beside a soldier of twenty-five. He had just married her and
was carrying her off to his village. Another time the bus
stopped in a melon field. The driver took a lot from the little
boy who was selling them, then walked away without pay-
ing; he was laughing. Afterwards some of the melons got
eaten, the rest were thrown out of the window.

India has always thirsted for God: it still does. I know that
Christ is there in India. But it is a Christ who is weeping,
suffering, looking for deliverance, because we ever crucify
him. We have nothing to offer the youth of the West except
pain, distress, and perhaps confusion as well. But I am looking, all the time I am looking. . . .

When I look at the world, I see men and nations greedy for
power. Yet 2000 years ago a man lived on the earth. He sought
no power. He united men in a single, universal body. What
have you done, you Westerners, claiming to be Christians,
with that seed that unites us? There are many ideas for
unity, but they are dogmatic and so can never be meeting-
points for all men. The Church is not an idea, it is love. This
is what makes it the final place on earth where the visible
unity of mankind can be realized.

AN END TO PRIVILEGES

Margarita

As a Latin-American, can I ask you, are you ready? Ready to give up the privilege of being rich people? Ready, for instance, to pay taxes, higher prices, to permit greater international justice? That means a huge effort of conscientization.* Are you ready to believe that there is not just one kind of development, the European kind, which must at all costs be exported and imposed elsewhere? Are you convinced that every people has to find its own, original ways towards liberation? Are you ready to become poor? Poor in the sense of realizing how much you need other people, conscious of having to receive from others, vulnerable? Are you ready to undergo a conversion in the sense of the revolution in your mentalities which will allow us to achieve our own revolution?

---

* *Conscientization:* awakening of consciousness in relation to environment and community and the development of a responsible and responsive attitude to their needs.

NEW SPIRITUAL DIMENSION

Geneva is at present working in journalism.
With others from Holland and England, she is a
member of a grass-roots community in Philadelphia, Pa.

As a young American woman I'm searching for a new spiritual depth to my existence. Somehow our technological society in the United States has robbed us from really experiencing the simple, human—yet mysterious—qualities of life. We are divided into isolated homes, private cars, fenced-off back yards, in front of our individual TV sets. For most people life has become a daily grind of working, eating, and sleeping, and there is little commitment to anything other than findings ways of escape from this awful rat-race. Through a shared life with others, I would like to break through some of these barriers of privatism so that together we could become a visible sign of the possibility of community.

TO BE OURSELVES

Isidore and Marie-Eugénie recently
completed their studies in Europe and
have returned to their home in Zaïre

The present generation in Africa is in real danger. We were
born at a time when colonization was carving up our ancestral heritage. We have hardly lived in our villages. Colonializa-
tion quickly made it its business to rid us of the authority of
the clan. Even our primary schooling took us beyond the
education of most of our parents. The result was that
from our earliest youth we were deprived of all traditional
guardianship. Indeed, blinded by our knowledge, our parents
often forgot that we needed their protection. So, from our
earliest youth we have had our destiny in our own hands,
or rather, we gave it over to strangers who felt themselves
in duty bound to make us 'white' so that we might become
'human'.

But the greatest drama of the African intellectual goes
even deeper. Cut off as we were from traditional Africa, the
only models we ever had were our European 'masters' whom
we wanted to resemble. The end result of this caused great
bitterness. If the black does not discover for himself that he
is making himself ridiculous, the white makes it his business
to bring it home to him that he is not what he should be.

Certainly, if our tradition still preserved all its solidity,
perhaps we wouldn't be so touchy in our relations with the
whites. The fact of being dispossessed makes us ill at ease and
we suspect (however unjustifiably) that we are constantly an
object of mockery.

Most of those who are disappointed with their experience
of Europe become nostalgic about traditional Africa (you can
even feel like this while living in the heart of Africa). Some
even speak of getting back to the sources; but their under-

taking is purely intellectual and in fact turns out to be equivocal.

Others, who attempt to live effectively according to our traditions, can't find their place in the new Africa which is fashioning itself on the image of Europe. In their childhood environment they become like notable visitors, and just cannot integrate themselves. When they try to live like every other native, and decide to renounce their status as 'white blacks', they are completely misunderstood by the majority of the people.

There, in a few words, is the situation in which we are living. As you can see, it is bewildering in its complexity. We cannot be 'ourselves', either with the whites or with our own people. For our own equilibrium, it is essential that we accept the fact that we are people who have been uprooted. Not to be aware of this, and refusing to accept it, means throwing open the door to all kinds of complexes. But even just accepting yourself as rootless is already a decisive step in the battle.

AN IMMIGRANT'S LETTER
FROM NEW YORK CITY

If an immigrant is a person who has left his native culture to enter another, then we are all immigrants in New York and, perhaps, America. We sit waiting for a new set of values, a new morality that will somehow make sense of the chaotic vacuum of our lives.

If I walk only a few blocks in New York, I see the immigrants clinging to their own moments of temporal happiness (happiness which can often be defined only as the absence of unendurable pain). I see the drug addicts at the corner with their glassy-eyed stares, waiting for the pusher so they can buy a few hours in which they can be oblivious to their own suffering. Sometimes they stand like vultures about to prey on some weak victim so that they can pay the price of admission for a moment of nirvana.

Walking farther I see the invisible old people. They are visible only to the vultures who, sensing their weakness, descend upon them to steal what little money they have and perhaps steal what little time they have left on earth. To everyone else they are invisible, for they have no power; their wisdom garnered from the past seems inapplicable in a world where one must keep abreast of the latest developments rather than reflect on the past. Memories are worthless in a time where only the future exists, yawning before us like a dark abyss.

I see the children wandering around aimlessly, something they have learned from their elders. By the time they are teenagers they will be middle-aged, and when they reach twenty they will be old. They seem to have learned nothing from their elders because their elders seem to have nothing to say except things like, 'You are the future' or 'I hope you'll find happiness whatever you do or wherever you go'. Their parents have abdicated and bestowed the sins of the world on their children, for them to correct. Nothing is more oppressive than suddenly being responsible for the world at the age of fifteen or sixteen. Who is strong enough to accept such a dubious gift? So the future of the world becomes scrawled on the walls of bathrooms and subway cars as an obscenity.

I walked by the Hare Krishnas selling magazines for a donation, a Marxist selling a paper for a donation, a blind alcoholic selling a 'thank you, good sir' for a donation which clinks in his metal cup. The papers at the corner stand say that rapes and murders are up 40% while car thefts are down by 33%. Congress is mad at the President; the President (whom no one ever sees) says we have won an honourable peace in Vietnam—after obliterating half the people there as well as any national conscience which remained. Those who spoke out have been jailed or become cynics in the land where everyone is free to disagree, but not to change government policy. One story says that all men are chauvinist and another says that everyone should become homosexual, which would somehow free both sexes from oppression. The price of gas is going up and the value of the dollar is going down, which means Volkswagens and Japanese televisions will be more expensive and for many people that long-awaited trip to the Carribbean, sexy Paris, historic Rome, fun-loving Munich, and sophisticated London will have to wait.

Finally I pass a church. I read the bulletin board outside. It says that everyone is welcome, but the door is locked. There is a wide selection of activities to choose from. There are three services, clubs for every age group, Bible study on Thursdays, and a Christian coffee house, where you can safely send your children, on Friday and Saturday night (thus freeing you to go out on the town). There is something for almost everyone, sort of a supermarket selection of the most 'relevant' activities for today's churchgoer. Alas, attendance is down 25% from ten years ago; perhaps a consultant should be hired to discern what the problem is.

Who is an immigrant in New York City? It would be better to ask if there is anyone who is not an immigrant. We are more alike in this city than we are like the land we have left (be it Puerto Rico, Haiti, Italy, Ireland, the South, or the Midwest). We have become something new and frightening. A modern day wanderer in the post-industrial, pre-technological no-man's land. We are different in our colour and amount of money we have in our wallet or checking account, but we are alike in our lostness. Some grope for dreams which they know have turned into nightmares for others. Somehow they hope that they will be different; that for them the great American dream will be filled with utopian pleasures. Others have given up even dreaming, for either they have reached the American dream and found it empty, or the pressures of everyday realities have made it impossible even to dream.

Yet perched here, an immigrant huddled with other immigrants, on the edge of the Apocalypse or the future (whichever you care to call it), there is some hope that Christ is with us. Yes, that Christ is *even* with us in the chaos of the American middle ages. It is often easier to see Christ in Africa, Asia, and South America than it is to see him here. Here we suffer as both oppressor and oppressed, caught in a spider web of our own making, not being able to move sometimes because of the fear of wrapping ourselves up even more in the fine thread. Somehow we must accept the fact that Christ can even take our sins upon himself and *even* free *us*! That itself is a form of humility we Americans have to learn; that our sins are not too large for God to forgive, because we are not greater than God.

Sincerely,
Tim

CONTEMPLATION:
WHERE LIFE BEGINS TO BE REAL

Klaus, from Stuttgart, Germany.
As a parish priest, he has been concerned
with immigrant workers

We constantly find ourselves back at the start, at the point where life begins to be real. Sometimes we are forced there, seemingly against our will. Or we regularly return, because how else shall we continue to grow? Each of us sooner or later discovers this, a reality set deep within himself—so deep that only he can reach it.

Suppose that we are running away from ourselves, or that we are involved in situations demanding the impossible: in the end we have to find a way back to ourselves. We burn after a happiness that is also liberation.

There are moments when we are several together, nothing being done or said: we are just there, in silence. Not embarassed silence, and not oppressive. Only, we realize then how useless is our eagerness to talk to others, always wanting to justify and defend our own positions. And that seems so unnecessary. Instead, we share all that we have no words or gestures to express. It means making room for patience, for expectancy. The result is an openness that carries us way beyond superficiality and agitation. We come nearer to expecting something quite new, as though we had some premonition then of a communion without limits. So at times, and with increasing frequency, we seek out opportunities of silence. Not emptiness, but a solitary encounter, inhabited stillness. Spaces unknown, scarcely entered upon previously; solitude with a familiar feel to it. Silence is not just something to be mastered.

Think of people in Taizé spending hours in church: What is each one trying to attain? What comes rising up?

Thoughts? Images? Dreams? Prayer? Conflict? Peace? Liberation? Pain? Joy? Silence is not easy.

When we are silent, what we encounter is not stillness but noise, the noise that exists in me. The unstable whirling-round, the unquietness is not simply round about me but also in me, and even stronger there. I try to still the manifold voices: memories, anguish, revolt. 'Thoughts are monkeys swinging through the branches of the mind.'

We are caught up in ourselves, not knowing what to say or where to turn. We are so alive, brimming over: people, images, old ways and new, confusion. It is already remarkable if we can resist our agitation and lay aside the usual thought process.

But we long to perceive something: to see, to hear. To hear a word coming to us from elsewhere.

Our search after contemplation is always threatened: there is anxiety that makes us stop, look backwards or inwards; there is our sentimentalism. Because contemplation is not withdrawing to inner planes of being, neither is it an island or a shrinking away from the evil world to enjoy on one's own an illusion of life.

Our quest in meditation is directed in the opposite direction: for a quality of liveliness that forms a living core at the very heart of our being. Searching for life, hungering after life; life to receive, life to give. And what we are seeking has one name in which everything is contained: Christ: 'I am the way, the truth and the life.'

Stillness before Christ is very human: the nearest thing to it would be friendship or love. Spending time together, just being there and waiting without any particular aim, free of everything. The simple fact of the other's presence is enough: life, joy. 'In every person there is a share of solitude that no intimacy can overcome.'

The stillness of contemplation opens our heart to something without limits: the life of those to whom I belong ineluctably; the questions of those people who do not believe and who deny or attack the Church; the pains of men imprisoned in oppression or bitterness. . . . There are all my questions to which I cannot return empty because I want them to be part of my life.

My life becomes a matter of new decisions. Living to what end? Working for what purpose? Why study? What point in struggling? Share what? What is my deep calling? The decision I have to make goes far beyond my reasoning, my strength, my imagining, my insights, my detailed analysis. Many possibilities, few things that I can work out and reinforce. Feeling my way forward, I seek to be firmly rooted in those depths where day after day, now painfully, now joyfully, I find life to draw on.

What is good? What is necessary? What is beautiful? Why am I here? What should I, can I, give my life for? The answer is not one that I can find in a moment's enthusiasm or in a burst of feeling. I will often turn to where I know I shall find simplicity and honesty with myself. And I see the world and the men who are my responsibility in a new way, sometimes—brighter for all their darkness and grief. Through the confusion passes the tender mercy of Christ, through all our guiltiness.

Silence is marked by constancy. We yearn after an underlying continuity, a 'moral memory' (Bonhoeffer) so we shall not simply forget or reject tomorrow the things that yesterday were for us good and full of hope. Justice, truth, beauty, like friendship, community, love, all need time and faithfulness. They demand stillness, expectancy, clarity. Those are signposts on our way.

TO IDENTIFY OURSELVES
WITH OUR PEOPLE

*Nestor and Olga were married just a few days
before setting out on a year of travelling
in preparation for the Council of Youth*

We come from Argentina. Seeing how our people live is a source of hope for us. The whole people of Latin America is increasingly aware of its development. In 1968 at Medellin, our bishops were already echoing wide-spread rejection of exploitation and of oppression due to vested interests and neo-colonialism.

Our hope resides in the fact that our people have become aware of their situation and have started to struggle: not to 'have more', in terms of consumer goods but to 'be more' by discovering the place of man in society and establishing more human conditions of living.

In *Populorum Progressio*, Paul VI spoke of conditions that are 'less human': the material needs of those deprived of the minimum necessary for life, the moral needs of men wounded by self-centred living, the oppressive structures growing out of every misuse of power, the exploitation of those who work; he insisted that we must pass to conditions that are 'more human' and can open on to belief: there man reaches his full humanity.

Today the crushed and oppressed are lifting up their voices and many of the young rally to them. Christians cannot but join this movement, even if it involves rejecting privileges and personal wealth for the benefit of the broader human community.

We are attempting to live a commitment for mankind and the struggle to which this leads stems from our faith: we feel strongly that we are led to this commitment by the fact of our belonging to the Church.

22

As soon as we say 'Church', questions and disagreements come surging up. Is it possible to struggle in order that man should no longer be victim of man and at the same time belong to the Church? We believe that the answer is 'Yes'.

We know that the Church, like us, is tainted with sin. But it matters to us. Our wish is to rebuild it, not destroy it: a renewed Church, that will not be turned in on itself, constantly striving to be more perfect, more beautiful . . . but that will be outward-looking, going towards men because it has discovered that its mission lies in that. . . . A Church in the form of a servant, taking the problems of all men and making them its own.

The Church is being born anew, is already growing, here in Latin America. It is already very much alive. Its birth is taking place amongst those people who are poorest and most oppressed. At the present time, to identify ourselves with our people as they struggle towards humanity because of what we believe : that is what we are searching for.

MAY CHRISTIANS NO LONGER BE BEARERS OF GOOD NEWS?

Brother Roger, Prior of Taizé

All through the summer of 1969, we were wondering about the wave of pessimism sweeping through the Church and almost tearing it apart. Attitudes like 'what is the use?' and 'that has all been done before' are enough to make people lose their footing and become discouraged, so great is the impact of bad news on the people of God.

I have been aware of the consequences of this for the past two years or so. Men and women who loved and served the Church with a real devotion have begun to have doubts. Others feel bound to take the opposite stance and engage in contemporary crusades. The sadness of this time robs us of any incentive to forge ahead.

What good news can be found to give fresh inspiration to the greatest number of people?

Joyful news for everybody

BEGINNING OUR PREPARATION

What are you searching for? Right round the world, people
are asking the kind of questions that Pierino and Geneva and
the others are asking. On every continent, from north of the
Arctic Circle in Finland to Melbourne, Australia . . . from
Bangalore, India, to Salem, Massachusetts . . . and from
Kyoto, Japan, to the northeast of Brazil, people are searching.
Individually and in cells and groups and small communities,
they are trying to respond to the questions that confront
them in their local situations: personal questions of faith
and belief and relationships with others, social and political
questions about man and his future and the way he is living
now, questions about the Church, and the way Christians
live together. They are joined together in their desire to
communicate with others, to live an ever deepening relationship of communion with them, and by the hope and support
they find in knowing that however difficult their situation,
they are not alone. The struggling and the searching are
being shared by all those who are involved in this time of
preparation leading us towards the worldwide Council of
Youth. The preparation began on Easter Day 1970, in Taizé,
France.

Taizé is a village, set on a hillside amidst the fields and vine-
yards of the rolling countryside between Chalon-sur-Saône
and Macon. On first sight, it is typical of the villages of the
region: a small cluster of tiled roofs, around a twelfth century church, built by the monks of Cluny. From 1940, it has
been the home of the community of brothers who have taken
'Taizé' as their family name.

'The Lord Christ, in his mercy and his love for you, has
chosen you to be a sign of brotherly love within the Church.
He wills that with your brothers you should realize the
parable of the community.' These words are read each time
a new brother makes his life commitment and they sum up

the aim of the brothers' life: for Christ, and because of him, to live a sign of community and reconciliation in an alienated and divided world.

When the Prior, Brother Roger, first came to Taizé not long after the start of World War II, he was alone. France was partitioned: Unoccupied France to the south, the Nazi-occupied zone to the north. The demarcation line between the two ran just north of Taizé and the situation of human distress and tension created by war was one of the factors that lay behind Brother Roger's choice of Taizé as a base for the future community. For two years, he used his home as a refuge for resistance workers and refugees, notably Jews, fleeing from the occupied zone towards Switzerland and freedom. When the Gestapo finally burst into the house in 1942, he was in Geneva, and for the next two years, any possibility of returning to Taizé was excluded. It was in Geneva that he was joined by the first brothers: in an apartment near the cathedral, they started working out their first steps in the common life. When they returned to Taizé at the liberation, they made contact with a camp for German prisoners in the region close by, and soon obtained permission for the prisoners to visit with them and to share in the community prayer. Receiving resistance workers at a time when many people were 'collaborating', and later receiving German prisoners in a France that had become strongly anti-Nazi is significant of the call to reconciliation of the Community right from the beginning: being open to everyone, seeking to love all men, especially the most underprivileged, whatever their background or position.

When the visitor arrives in Taizé today, he is struck by the central place given to common prayer. Rising above the hill is the Church of Reconciliation, built in 1962 by German Christians as a sign of reconciliation after the War. Three times a day, the bells summon the brothers and all those visiting the community, to gather together for the Office. Morning, noon, and evening, the Office is a time of celebration which permits us to sing together or, in silence, to allow ourselves to be penetrated by the Word of God. The essential is quite simply being there, in the presence of God, expressing ourselves through our bodies, standing, kneeling, seated . . . or there are even times when the organ alone gives voice to our waiting and searching.

For these times of common prayer everything—work, discussion, activity—stops; not to be forgotten, but to be drawn together, with all the tensions and struggle and joy of daily life, and to be situated in the perspective of the Gospel. The shocks and conflicts which we meet, and the suffering and incomprehensibility of the world are brought to the light of Christ, who in turn sends us out again to discern his life and his presence in the life of men.

The common service of Christ to which the brothers are committed is expressed in vows of celibacy, community of goods, and the acceptance of an authority.

CELIBACY: to be available for Christ and his Kingdom, 'can be accepted only so as to give yourself more completely to your neighbour with the very love of Christ'.

THE COMMUNITY OF GOODS is total and involves not only material goods, but spiritual and intellectual as well. From the start, the brothers have never accepted gifts for themselves, but, like a family, they work to earn their living. There is a printing and publishing house, as well as ceramics workshops. Some brothers write, others have jobs in the region: one is teaching computer science in the technical college in Cluny; two others are an architect and a plumber, whilst a third is involved in a co-operative farm, the Copex, started jointly by the Community and several village families as an effort to resolve some of the economic problems of the immediate neighbourhood.

'THE MINISTRY OF AUTHORITY IS A MINISTRY OF COMMUNION.' The brothers see the Prior's ministry as pastoral, that of constantly drawing the community together, listening to everyone and stimulating the community in its search to be 'of one heart and one mind'.

The brothers come from a dozen different countries and from many different denominations, including, with the agreement of the Archbishop of Paris, Roman Catholics. In their desire to live a parable of community, they are attempting to promote the visible unity of all Christians. This means involvement in the life of different Churches: one brother works with SODEPAX, the commission on Society, Development, and Peace at the World Council of Churches in Geneva, another is the Prior's representative to the Holy See. Above all, it means that the search for unity is not an abstraction, concerned only with ideas and discussions, but involves the very life process of the community itself.

It means, too, that the unity they are seeking does not stop at Christians, for the Church is not an end in itself, it exists for mankind. The single aim of visible unity between Christians is to make the Church more credible. How can the Church become a ferment of unity, a place of communion that is open to everyone, where all men may be welcome and be at ease? Brother Roger has written, 'Ecumenism is quite simply the receiving of everyone'.

THE ORIGIN OF AN INTUITION

People have been coming to Taizé for years now. Young people from every geographical, political, and religious background have gathered in international encounters, finding hospitality, prayer, being listened to.

It became clear to some of us that we were not there simply on our own behalf, but that those of us who were there represented others, that we had aspirations that were shared by a great many people.

It was becoming clear too, that while it was good to be able to meet together for a week of sharing our searching and commitments and experiences, this was not enough. There was always the problem of what happened when the meeting was over and we separated and went home. It became more and more urgent to find a way of supporting one another, of staying together while geographically far apart, and above all, accomplishing some kind of common gesture in the world for our fellow men.

Brother Roger was well aware of these questions, and in February, 1969, he noted in his journal:

And now, during these days, young people from forty-two countries are gathered here, quite unexpectedly, in the depth of winter. We are exploring together. Forty-two countries: we are experiencing a kind of little council of youth.

These young people shun privileges for themselves, and equally they cannot stand any caste-mentality. With them, the Church will go far.

And in June the same year:

For months past, one thing has been preoccupying me: with the present discord in the Church, what act could give peace to those who are shaken and strength to those who are committed? I sense that such an act should be a gathering of an exacting nature, regularly repeated for the years to come. Over a certain period of time, building and searching together. And with that, again and again the same thought dominates: this demanding gathering is going to be a council of youth. But who will carry it out? As far as we are concerned, there is no comparison between the effort needed and our possibilities.

Besides, if we set out in that direction, what trials lie in store. Oppositions are bound to arise, and peace and friendship are valuable beyond price. Where to draw new courage?

Can men dare to hope today? This was the theme of the summer meetings in 1969. Is it possible to hope and to go on hoping, in a world that is so scarred by every kind of injustice and selfishness and despair. . . .?

It was hope and how difficult it is for so many people to be able to hope that led to the suggestion of an announcement to be made on Easter Day 1970—'Joyful News' which would transcend the pessimism and discouragement and trials of the present time and bring back joy to the Church.

As we listened to one another, we discovered that the question which we were asking was basically the question which Christ asked the people he met, What are you seeking?

Furthermore, the news that came on the first Easter morning and which completely turned all man's wisdom upside down, is still true for us. Why do you seek the living among the dead? How can we discover the Risen Christ at the heart of our own situations?

The 'Joyful News' that was finally announced in 1970 was the outcome of experiences collected from all over, of letters from round the world, and of a team of youth from all the continents. On Easter Day, an Intercontinental Team spoke before a gathering of 2500 young people from 35 countries who, by their presence, represented in a sense all those who are seeking to root their lives in the Gospel and to build a world of justice.

Before the actual announcement, the Team explained how it

had been worked out, and how its inspiration came from the southern continents :

Last year, we decided to announce from Taizé, on Easter Day 1970, some joyful news for young people: a challenge of hope in this troubled time in the Church, in these times when whole sections of humanity are alienated by the forces of oppression, in these times when the intolerable privileges of some deprive others of their very awareness of being men.

We have been attentive to the suggestions of youth from all five continents. We have grasped the fact that for a very large number, there exists a thirst for God, but, at the same time, the will to move forward in the service of mankind. For them, it is all or nothing. When they understand Christ, it is as the Christ 'who is our life'. When they understand the Church, they wish her to be a creative force.

What we have understood most clearly is that people are waiting for a quite new and different project that will commit them totally for Christ, which sets free their energies and which will prepare within them an outburst of creativity so that the world may be made fit to live in. Then, the violence of hatred can still be changed into the 'violence of the peace-maker'.

In order to find the news that was most desired, we listened, thought, and prayed. In our concern for reciprocity between the two hemispheres, the essential in what we have grasped comes from the southern continents. Young Latin-Americans have felt 'the urgent necessity for a Church which is more and more paschal, which refuses every means of power, and is a faithful witness to a Gospel which sets men free' (Medellin Conference 1968). Africans and Asians find themselves turned away by the Northern Hemisphere from the values of communion, sharing and also of festival which are theirs.

In our search for a way to answer their hope, at a time when the Church is going through a desert, and when the earth is becoming uninhabitable for many, we called to mind the first Christians. At the beginning, 'they held everything in

33

common, they were of one heart and spirit' and their brotherly unity could be seen. When their unanimity disappeared, when tensions developed into divisions, they decided to meet together in order to maintain communion and avoid breaking apart. The news then that we are announcing is an Easter message. Here it is:

The Risen Christ comes to quicken a festival
in the innermost heart of man.

He is preparing for us a springtime of the
Church: a Church devoid of means of power,
ready to share with all, a place of visible
communion for all humanity.

He is going to give us enough imagination
and courage to open up a way of reconciliation.
He is going to prepare us to give our life so
that man be no longer victim of man.

(Intercontinental Team: Easter 1970)

That Easter Day, once the young people had finished, Brother Roger continued:

In order to live this Joyful News,
a way, an instrument, has been found,
and I will announce it to you:
We are going to hold a worldwide
Council of Youth.

AN EVENT IN THE LIFE
OF THE CHURCH

'If anyone had asked me when I came out of the church on Easter Day 1970, what all that meant, I wouldn't have been able to reply, because I hadn't understood,' Angelina says now. 'I only knew that all this corresponded to something deep inside me, even if I could not express it. I had sensed a common hope with many other young people gathered at Taizé. On that day there was only one word in everyone's hearts: "hope".'

It is difficult to understand straightaway because it will be the first time in history that there has been a council of youth. We must bring it to birth together with the patience that great things require.

Three weeks after Easter, the Pope, speaking about ecumenism at the Sunday Angelus in St Peter's Square, said, *We look toward Taizé with respectful attention.* At Epiphany 1971, Paul VI telegraphed to Brother Roger, *Holy Father very touched by message of numerous young people preparing Council of Youth at Taizé: deeply grateful: calls God's blessing on generous participants.*

Dr Eugene Carson Blake, then General Secretary of the World Council of Churches, attended the announcement of the Council of Youth. He was back in Taizé at Easter 1971 and before his visit at Easter 1972, he declared in a public statement: *My attendance at the Youth Meeting you are preparing for Easter will be my fourth visit to Taizé within the space of a year. I appreciate your community's efforts to overcome the present ecumenical deadlock, all that you have undertaken with tens of thousands of young people all over the world, and your efforts to participate in the search for greater justice among men.*

As for Patriarch Athenagoras, of Constantinople, the great

concern, right up to the time of his death, was that of the eucharist. At the end of Brother Roger's last visit to him, in the doorway, he made yet again the gesture of raising the chalice. *The cup and the breaking of bread. Remember, there is no other solution.*

Basically the Council will be an event in the life of the Church. That is what the word 'council' itself attempts to show. The members of the Intercontinental Team wondered whether other terms would not better translate our aspirations. They discussed it at great length, until finally they came to realize that this is the only word which satisfies all that we were trying to express.

Through a council we are hoping to live, for several years, *an event in the Church.* Not some meeting or a movement, but explicitly an event in the Church, for mankind.

The term 'council' expresses also the *provisional aspect* which is important for us: it evokes an event which will last for several years, but which will have a beginning and an end, leaving open the possibility of living something quite different afterwards.

A council will lead us *to live a communion in a universal way,* coming from every country with the contributions and questioning of our different origins and cultures, anxious not to exclude anybody.

Consequently it could be one of the ways of contributing to a new breakthrough in the ecumenical vocation of Christians: to help Christians to find again a brotherly communion to make the Church more credible to men. Perhaps it might be a way of answering a question which has been much asked and which Brother Roger expressed like this:

When faced with the fact that very many young people reject the Church, why stand still to interpret that pessimistically, anxiously or even polemically? Is not the main thing to question ourselves thoroughly so as to discern beyond the immediate event the signs—already visible—of a springtime of the Church?

The idea of a Council of Youth arose out of a failure: the dead end to which the Ecumenical Movement has come.

After years of good ecumenical work, which has had its results, hadn't we come to a standstill? In this situation I asked myself the question: what can we do? Ecumenism has reached a ceiling. Who will make the break-through?

CENTRED ON THE RISEN CHRIST

A council, whatever else it may be, is always a common celebration of the Risen Christ, and an invocation of the Holy Spirit.

On the evening of Easter Day 1970, we made a start to this celebration, meditating in the Church of Reconciliation on a text which is fundamental to the whole of the preparation:

WE CELEBRATE THE RISEN CHRIST IN THE EUCHARIST. By it we are given to share in the life of the risen Christ and to participate in the paschal mystery: to share in the trials of Christ who, until the end of time, suffers in his body, the Church, and in men, our brothers: to live at the deepest levels within ourselves the festival always offered by the risen Christ, he who alone transfigures the depths of man. The eucharist is there for us who are weak and defenceless. We receive it in a spirit of poverty and in repentance of heart. In our journey through the desert towards a Church of sharing, the eucharist gives us courage not to store up manna, to give up material reserves and to share not only the bread of life but also the goods of the earth.

WE CELEBRATE THE RISEN CHRIST BY OUR LOVE FOR THE CHURCH, a love that kindles a fire on the earth. If the Church is in one way like an underground river which, in a hidden, secret movement, assures a continuity that flows from the very first Pentecost, it is also a 'city set on a hill to be seen by all men'. By the visibility of our brotherly love, by our rediscovered unity, the Church is called to become an unparalleled ferment of fraternity, of communion, of sharing, for all humanity: that is the essence of its ecumenical vocation. On the eve of his death Christ prayed that our unity would make it possible for men to believe.

WE CELEBRATE THE RISEN CHRIST IN MAN OUR BROTHER. Living

by prayer and by confidence in one another—poor values—
we discover that man is 'sacred by the wounded innocence
of his childhood, by the mystery of his poverty'. In man we
see the very face of Christ, 'above all when tears and suffering
have made this face more transparent'. So we will give even
our life that man be no longer victim of man.

THOSE WHO BELIEVE
THOSE WHO SEEK

Celebrate the Risen Christ!

Many say: *It is foolhardy to want to believe nowadays in the resurrection of Christ and to say so.* To seek to believe. . . . Yes, but feeling our way, sustained, nourished each by the faith of the others. That is what we are all trying to live, far from thinking that we have reached the goal.

Faith in the Risen Christ makes us penetrate the hidden depths of our relationship with all other people. The limit of faith is one of the most mysterious there are. The believer and the non-believer exist within us at the same time. That is the reason why the Joyful News does not wish to create a split or a distinction between believers and non-believers. On the contrary, it is a call to seek together.

The non-believers and members of other religions who feel themselves called by it are numerous. *I do not really know who the Risen Christ is,* say some, *but reconciliation, the struggle that man should no longer be the victim of man, all that says a great deal to me.*

They question us, they ask us, we who call ourselves Christians, whether we are really living all the consequences of our faith, particularly in an active concern for justice.

But they in their turn are questioned too. When they hear the challenge of the Joyful News, they can better grasp just how far faith in the Risen Christ goes. As a young Latin-American said: *If that is really what Christians want to live, then, religion will no longer be the opium of the people, but the ferment of liberation.*

A young Muslim from North Africa wrote, a few days after Easter 1970: *At Taizé I was able to speak of everything, of the future of men, of religions and of what they have in common. Races, languages, and divisions no longer existed. I would have liked to speak in Arabic, to describe my thoughts* on the Risen Christ. For me as a Muslim, Christ is also risen. He will return again at the end of time. What is needed now is a young generation which frees itself from closed traditions, and who desire an understanding between all men. Where can we begin? In the Church, for she is already a bond between Christians of different countries. I promise you to discuss this with practising Muslims and to challenge them to be more open, and to try to understand that Christ rose for everyone. I will begin with young people, so that they may know that at least there is a possibility of coexistence with Christians.

A COUNCIL OF THINGS TO COME

In the complementary relationship between the generations, young people have an irreplaceable part to play for the Church. They carry within them the promise of a different world. Through them, the future exists in embryo : the Council of Youth is also the Council of things to come.

The Spirit passes on to the Churches a specific message through the younger generation. There are aspects of the Gospel which young people grasp perhaps more directly and which they can explain to everyone.

Youth carries on its shoulders an enormous responsibility, said Dom Helder Camara. *When one travels through the world, in rich countries and in poor countries, in countries of the East, and the West, everywhere one meets this demanding youth. A demand, first of all, for authenticity; on parents, teachers, pastors. A demand above all on themselves. This youth which, in the world of today, hungers and thirsts for justice, urgently needs to be understood, to find understanding, real understanding.*

In families, in churches, in schools a great deal is spoken about dialogue, but how difficult it is really to understand young people. Roger with this luminous idea of a Council of Youth seems to me to give us all an example of understanding and confidence in young people.

The Council of Youth will be composed of a majority of young people, but in order to avoid all segregation, older people, elderly people, and even children will also take part.

The Council should allow young people to put themselves in a position to listen to the oppressed, the very poor, in the Southern Hemisphere as in the Northern Hemisphere, and to prepare themselves to give their own life. It should help them to give their full measure, to set free all their creativity for Christ, for the Church, for men.

Ricky, a black from Dallas, Texas, writes:

The Council of Youth is for me the beginning of a new world. The beginning of a totally new way of life. In short, the beginning of real change for all of us, not just a privileged few. For me, young people are the beginning of this real change.

In Taizé, the light of the world has been given to young people, for this is the light of the future. This light contains the willingness to love and the courage to hope. And the glow of this fire will shine so bright in the world of darkness, that it will truly light the world.

At present the Council is still in preparation, and soon it will begin, and I believe it will be a place of hope for all oppressed people, a place where all oppressed people can lay down their burdens. I believe it should be a place of community-love, a place where people are helping one another, supporting one another.

A place where people should be willing to lay down their lives, if need be, for one another: where brotherhood is reality and not just a hopeless dream.

According to an ancient Chinese proverb, a journey of 1000 miles begins with a single step. The young people in the preparation for the Council have made that first step, a step toward a future of hope and a world of light.

A LONG MARCH

On Easter Day 1970 the young people of the Intercontinental Team concluded as follows:

The Council of Youth has now been announced. It will begin later, it will be the second stage. As it is impossible to achieve anything worthwhile without a minimum period of preparation, it is necessary, before attempting to come together in council, to meditate and to live: to live the festival, to live communion and sharing, 'hoping beyond all hope'. At this moment, we are entering upon the preparation for the Council, during which each of us will try to experience life, starting out from our inner poverty, but towards the Risen Christ, this lamp lighting the depths of our darkness.

And so the preparation began. The search goes on from continent to continent. The first links were formed, like a garland going round the world. Taizé has been as a sounding board or a catalyst or an antenna relaying all that is gradually maturing here and there, in more or less explicit fashion. We have begun 'a long march through the desert: setting out without knowing our destination, waiting for the fulfilment of a promise'. Year by year we have been able to deepen our awareness of the implications of the Joyful News.

The long march towards the opening of the Council of Youth was to last four years, from Easter 1970 till mid-1974, although we did not know this at the beginning. After two years of intensive preparation, it became clear that the process could be accelerated and that the Council (which will itself last several years) could begin in two years' time.

Here is part of Brother Roger's statement at Easter 1972:

The point of gradually entering on an interior adventure is to prepare ourselves to live together an adventure in public. This means having the courage to take great risks.

The end point of this daring adventure is this: after listening to and summing up all the innumerable intuitions of very many young people, I am now able to announce to you that in two years' time, in 1974, the worldwide Council of Youth will begin.

Setting out
not knowing where we are to go

But what does this Joyful News really mean?
What are its implications in our lives?

Many people discover they have been living it 'unawares',
even if they have never heard of the Joyful News as such.
It echoes the voice of those who are giving their lives for the
liberation of man and of those who are struggling for the
rebirth of the Church. It expresses the hopes of those who are
exploited and oppressed.

The Joyful News puts into words what many people are
attempting to live, while at the same time it questions our
lives and provokes us to thought and action:

To set out, not knowing where we are to go

AN INTERIOR ADVENTURE

The preparation for the Council of Youth will be a long march through the desert:
setting out without knowing where it will lead us,
waiting for the fulfilment of a promise,
not letting ourselves get settled down.

In the aridity of the desert,
there is the freshness of the oasis.
There, we shall dig down together,
to find the water of life,
the festival in our hearts,
the surging spring that fills us.

It is this festival that we are called on to live
so as to set out . . .
To discover the living water,
we begin by plunging into the hidden
underground movement of the Church.

For the Church is a subterranean river,
forming an unbroken continuity with the first Pentecost,
and, at the same time, it is
'a city set on a hill, to be seen by all men'.

We are beginning by an exploration, in depth,
convinced that the living water will flow;
whent the spring surges up,
nothing can hold it back;
and the day will come when it bursts forth from the ground.

But this is not just any kind of march: the goals we have set ourselves cannot be achieved as if by magic. The times of achievement and conquest and arrival have to be prepared for, before joy and fraternity can explode. Each obstacle has to be met, one by one; pushing forward, being forced to fall back; slowly, the adventure together calls forth unknown strength from us; trust and confidence grow.

The 'obvious' way to start out would have been to hold congresses and assemblies, to draw up resolutions and issue manifestos and proclamations. But that would have been to take the easy way out. To begin in that way would have been to run the risk of achieving only words that are not rooted in the reality of men's lives and experience. So, we started the other way round. We have begun quite simply by living: living this interior adventure which finds its source in the depths of ourselves, and which will lead us, in a second stage, to a public adventure which will be the Council itself. In other words, we started out without having any idea of what the Council itself would be!

'But how can you prepare for something when you do not know what that something is?' One evening in Cincinnati, Ohio, a group were discussing this:

But you have got to have some idea of what it will be!

But, of course. We are searching, exploring, trying to live out the Joyful News, each one in his own situation, right round the world. Everybody, each person and each people of the world has something unique to contribute. The Council will be the pooling of all these experiences. After the years of questioning, the time will come to put together what we are finding, in a more explicit way...'

'Yes, but it all sounds so vague! How is it going to be organized?'

Then a stranger who had sat quietly through the whole discussion spoke up. A girl from Argentina:

'I know why you cannot understand!'
Silence.
'Because you are rich!'
'But what has that to do with it?'

51

'Because in your country, you have become used to having everything you want, straight away, programmed and packaged. You talk about the "instant society", and it is true! In my country, things are not like that at all. If you really want something, you know you can't get it straight away. So you start by putting a little aside. Later on, you put something else aside, and so on. . . And in this way, what you are looking for is preparing itself! It is the same with the Council of Youth'.

The preparation for the Council of Youth is not abstract or 'intellectual'. It begins by taking a hard look at the life we are leading. In all the questions that confront me and other men, where do I find the strength and the courage to make decisions and choices? Preparing for the Council, is first of all looking deep down within ourselves: living a period of inner liberation: letting the Joyful News penetrate the very roots of our being, so that it changes our lives inwardly and makes us take our stand in the struggles of mankind today.

An interior adventure does not mean over-introspection. On the contrary, it means searching for a stable centre, a source, which permits us to see the problems of life and the world more clearly, and to act.

Thus prayer becoming not just a step or stage in the long march, but an essential dimension throughout . . . letting Christ penetrate the heart of our existence, made up as it is of struggle and tension, love and hope. And it is in this way, that we discover the ability to create all things anew, as we fix our sight on the human face of Christ, we discover the 'newness' that wells up inside us.

And in all this adventure, wherever we are, in whatever country or continent, we are dependent on all the others. As each one of us pursues his own line of research to its conclusion, we shall be able to discover ways of bringing men together in a new relationship of communion. There are times on the long march when we come to a halt; to meet together, and in these times, we are discovering that the communion we are trying to create has already begun.

Joseph, from Kinshasa, expressed this one evening in Taizé:

I have discovered a lot of people through personal contact. Perhaps I had already exchanged views in a group, about the consumer society, the Third World, church institutions. But when one starts talking face to face, quite unsuspected aspects of the preparation of the Council begin to appear. I noticed that beneath the actual words of the Joyful News, there is a sort of current flowing through each one of us which grasps the very root of our being. The problems which we seem to discuss in a theoretical manner are painfully experienced within each of us. How each of us is determined to commit himself realistically, in one way or another, to fight against the oppression in our society. It is quite striking to meet one another on this level. . . Be it only to know that this Council which will grow round the Risen Christ is already of major importance in other people's lives.

The weeks of international meetings that are held in Taizé throughout the summer are times when you can share with many other people, and at the same time deepen your own interior awareness. Perhaps what we tell you about them here will help those who can never go to Taizé to join in this long march in their turn. . .

A WEEK IN TAIZE

Monday afternoon. . .

'Ya, uit Nÿmegen. We zÿn vanmorgen om zes uur vertrokken. . .' Tu vienes de Barcelona? No es posibile!' Jacques! Ou est-ce que tu as laissé les sacs?. . . De que barrio? . . . uno dei fratelli è italiano. . . Bitte? . . . Die Namen? . . . The reception tent is crowded. It is a bit of a shock to find that everybody does not speak English! And there are so many people. Is this yet another anonymous crowd?

'Hi, there! Where are you from?'

It's hot, and we've been hitch-hiking since yesterday morning.

'Here! Have something to drink.'

A wide empty space in front of the Church of Reconciliation, and there are tents all around. Big ones and small ones, all in different colours. To one side, rows of marquees, used for meetings. To the other, a silent area, where there is no music and no conversation.

'What kind of meeting do you want to take part in?' In fact, there are several different kinds, all going on at one time, Meetings where there is a minimum of discussion, for people who want to be quiet: for people who are here for the first time: meetings for those who have been involved in the preparation for the Council for some time and want to review and deepen their experience.

By Monday night, everyone has made his choice on how he wants to spend the week. There are two different languages per tent and the meetings get under way. There are around fifty people in each group, and they are led by members of the youth team who have prepared the week.

First, introductions.

Why are we here?

What do we expect from this week?

In just over half an hour, the first meeting breaks up into small groups of seven or eight people. These groups will meet together every day, for discussion, relaxation, manual work, and other activities. The accent is on the sharing of life and experience, rather than on debating who is 'right'.

No, this is not an anonymous crowd. Gradually, the barriers come down among the group members. Gradually, 'black' and 'white', 'German' and 'Italian', 'foreigners', 'Catholic', 'Protestant', the 'non-Christian', are discovered as people. A sense of communion emerges. Each person represents something like a question for the others. . .

'. . . . .We are often astonished by the ease with which young Europeans talk about the Third World . . . development and under-development, liberation, aid and revolution . . . Why do they talk so much about the Third World? . . . Do they believe that this makes them revolutionaries? . . .'

. . . The bells . . .

Seigneur, ouvre mes lèvres,
  Et ma bouche publiera ta louange.
O Dieu, viens à mon aide,
  Seigneur, à mon secours.

The camp-site has gone quiet. Everybody has gathered in the church for the Office.

'Perhaps it is the silence that is most impressive of all.'
'But what do you do during the silence?'

Even outside the prayer times, the church remains a place of silence. A large, enclosed space, almost without furniture . . . the light, filtered by the coloured glass, changes through the day . . . people . . . quiet . . . waiting . . . sitting . . . kneeling . . . lying face downwards on the floor . . .

At the noon prayer, the silence is broken by the low chanting of the Alleluia :

Al - le - lu - ia, al - le - lu - ia, al - le - lu - - ia

while a text for meditation is read :

> *Remember Jesus Christ,*
> *Risen from the dead.*
> *If we have died with him,*
> *we shall also live with him;*
> *if we endure,*
> *we shall also reign with him;*
> *if we deny him,*
> *he will also deny us;*
> *if we are faithless,*
> *he remains faithful—*
> *for he cannot deny himself.*
> *This word is sure.*

'You know, the really amazing thing is that there are so few brothers! That church must have two thousand people in it. And there they are, just a tiny handful in the middle. And somehow, there is a unity that flows through everyone.'

Every week, different aspects of the Joyful News are examined in 'workshops' that come together several times : contemplation and the struggle for mankind; giving our lives through trade union, political and professional commitment; believing in the resurrection; living in the happiness of the Beatitudes in our society; what can Christian and non-Christian mean for one another?; learning to share between people of different backgrounds and cultures.

Evenings are taken up with different activities, sometimes discussion of issues raised during the week . . . opportunities

to sit down and meet with people from other continents . . .
people with a special interest to share . . . or relaxing together
with music and singing and mimes and poetry . . .

Here is Joseph, from Zaïre, describing the theatre workshop
he has been leading:

*We have been using as many different forms of expression
as possible: gestures, objects, shouts, complaints, laughter.
Silence and expression through movement are just as much
part of someone's personality as his words.*

*You can take over somebody's ideas, but you cannot copy
his way of laughing. Peoples' faces do not lie: they are what
they are. When a man is seeking reconciliation with others,
he must learn to reconcile himself with his own body and all
its parts. The body weighs us down, whereas it should carry
us.*

*Through the summer, different themes drawn directly or
indirectly from the Joyful News are handled in theatrical
form by the various groups. The expression given to each
theme varies according to the group.*

*Among the best of these has been the representation of
contemporary society through a game made up of people
dressed in large hoods on which were written 'school', 'ad-
ministration', 'factory', 'motorway', etc. They are all bound
together by a cord which in turn binds them to a principal
character. This is an image of alienation. At a given moment,
the principal offers a hood to a young man, who gets up. Here
is youth, to whom society is offering a place in the system.
He tries to slip into the hood, but it is too tight. So he tears
it in pieces and takes up a sling which he uses to throw a stone
at the principal character. As the principal falls to the
ground, the others are set free. Hoods and cords are thrown
aside and everyone joins a circle. Singing and dancing express
the hope that comes with liberation.*

*Another theme that is much used is the Tower of Babel.
All the actors form a pyramid. Someone climbs to the top:
here is man who wants to outdo himself, the epitome of*

human pride. Then everything collapses and confusion reigns. It is impossible to understand each other, even among those who speak the same language. Someone who says, 'I'm hungry', is greeted with 'What? I don't understand!' Non-communication goes far beyond mere language. Then along comes a poor man holding a piece of bread. He meets a woman who is even poorer than himself and he shares his bread with her. As they eat, they both notice that the other actors have nothing, so they start sharing the bread with them. Everyone is happy, in this act of sharing . . . until they notice the spectators . . . and so the sharing goes on. . . . Joy is impossible without sharing.

In my own opinion, the best thing of all is not only the fact that we manage to express ourselves in this way, even those who have never tried it before; it is the level of under-standing that is reached, and the communion that is created through these symbols and gestures.

Leaving our homes to go to Taizé we lived a death . . . our death. We dealt with this in saying that we were preparing 'to give our life so that man be no longer victim of man'. Then, learning to share self with other people . . . was a rising from the dead. There we were in Taizé to make other people aware of our problems and to become aware of theirs.

Through the searching together, we became strong, we began to want to return to our everyday situations so as to share the Joyful News with our brothers. This desire became a challenge during the last days we spent together. We came face to face with the challenge when we left the plane: in Chicago, New York, Mobile, Boston. We were no longer a group; on our own, we had to follow this challenge to the hilt.

FROM ONE EASTER TO THE NEXT

In our journey through the desert, the celebration of Easter forms an important stop over.

Each year, the individual routes of many people come together at that point, like a kind of oasis where we can sit down together to share, to widen our horizons, and then set off again. In this way, through exchange of experiences and through celebrating the Risen Christ together. It has been possible to indicate the particular aspect of the Joyful News to be explored through the coming year. Every Easter, an Intercontinental Team has traced out its main lines.

After 'festivity', following Easter 1970, came 'giving one's life so that man be no longer victim of man' in 1971. That year, the facade of the Church of Reconciliation at Taizé had to be demolished and a huge circus tent added onto the front of the church in order to accommodate the 7000 people who attended the meeting.

At Easter 1972, 16,000 young people heard the news that the Council would open during the summer of 1974. It was fantastic to look back on all that had been achieved during the previous two years and to look forward to the next two, where the whole thrust of the preparation was to be intensified, no matter the risks involved, in the knowledge that 'the Risen Christ will give us enough imagination and courage to become signs of contradiction according to the Gospel.

These are the themes, like guide lines, that run right through the whole of the preparation, in our home situations and in the meetings in Taizé.

But really, they are not 'themes' at all. Rather, they are questions about the way we live.

What does 'festival' mean for you?

How can we 'give our lives' for others?

How can we become signs of contradiction according to the Gospel?

Each one of us has to reply to these questions for himself.

We quote here just a few echoes of some people's thinking. Perhaps they will stimulate you to think about your own response, and that in turn will stimulate others.

FESTIVAL AND STRUGGLE

FESTE, FIESTA, FETE, FESTA, FESTIVAL . . .
the word exists in every language. In every country and civilization, festivals and celebrations take place.

What does it mean for you? What springs to mind when we talk about festivity? What do you celebrate in your life?

What are the obstacles and the barriers to festivity within us and round about us?

Is there such a thing in our daily existence as a festival that forms a point to which we can constantly return, especially when the going is rough, and which enables us to get started again?

And how can we communicate this festival to other people?

How difficult it is for many people in the Northern Hemisphere even to conceive of festivity and celebration other than as escape hatches from the real business of living. We do use the words, of course; but what has happened to the reality behind them? As an Anglican bishop commented, *We talk about a celebration of Holy Communion, but so often it is anything but!* Things were not always like this, however; in sixteenth-century Europe, there were nearly three-hundred feast days a year! We are sceptical when we hear of the fiestas and carnivals of South America. These are, after all, 'underdeveloped countries'! But in our northern civilization of production and efficiency and organization, are we still really sure that ours is the only answer for living? 'What does it profit a man to gain the whole world . . . ?'

Here, Justine, from Zaïre, shares something of what festivity means in Africa:

The African festival is always a manifestation of life in its intensity. The birth of a child brings young and old together; a marriage is an invitation to sing and dance; a friend's return from a far off country calls forth the rhythm of tom-tom and bells, of hands and feet. Life evokes festival, to relate the present to past and future. The festival is a springboard from which to launch out into the future.

There is no festival without others, and, if possible, all the others, for it is also the celebration of a communion, leading to fuller awareness of this basic reality. It is the occasion offered to everyone to feel the richness of total living, such as you feel when you are dancing and singing and vibrating together. Festival is a song of life, it celebrates the reconciliation between individuals and families and clans; it is the joy of brothers who are together again at last.

The history of mankind is made up of struggles, of adversities, even of cruelty . . . . . life demands that these be assumed and integrated into the current that flows toward the future. When the time of festival comes, the cares of each day vanish in self forgetfulness. For the Christian, the festival is the certainty that Jesus Christ has taken our human feasts and raised them to the level of his Risen Life. Christ quickens a festival in us from morning till night; his presence makes us overcome the wear and tear of time and the monotony of existence, because he has hold on our lives. The Christian festival is wholly compatible with suffering and struggle. The Christian who is deeply committed to life always has an inner hope. Therefore, he can vibrate with joy. Living the festival means communicating with the whole Christ living in us; it means living the joyous anticipation of his return.

'I work in a factory which makes electronic equipment. I assemble parts for television aerials. In the factory situation, living the festival means struggling for fairer wages and a better understanding between workers and owners. I do not think the word 'festival' is out of place, even in a factory.

There is no doubt about it: when I try to discover what prevents festival it is much easier to make a list of ways in which I am oppressed rather than the ways in which I oppress others. But we must be honest; each of us is both victim and oppressor.

What are the sources of oppression?

They are interior—prejudices, egoism, fear. And exterior—propaganda, publicity, exploitation, the restrictiveness of systems which stifle man rather than fulfil him.

How can we create living conditions which allow all men to be fully human? How, in the Northern Hemisphere, can we free ourselves so that festival, real liberation, may be possible for other people? How can we make our environment —family, work, school, church, trade union, political party —communities where a liberating festival exists?'

For me, living the festival is struggling. Struggling to make the Church truly a place and sign of reconciliation. Although I am often confused and sometimes disgusted by the hierarchy and institutions of the Church, I cannot live my faith outside it. I refuse uniformity and I think that the new Church will emerge from the present confrontations and questionings. But for that to happen we must be prepared to be part of the Church, to stay there and fight.

And I struggle too for men. I realize that the main injustices in this world are of a political nature, and so I am trying to analyse society politically, to understand the bases of injustice and to fight at this level. As a Christian I cannot just opt out saying, for example, that politics are rotten and that nothing can be done. . . . . Besides being the motivation for my commitment, Christ brings me hope.

THAT MAN BE NO LONGER
VICTIM OF MAN

How can we analyse and become conscious of all the situations where man is victim?

There are so many things that shackle man instead of making him free. We are accomplices in this. How can we change this process? What are the means of liberation?

How can we be consistent in our concern for mankind, even to the point of giving our life?

After a year of exploring the meaning of the festival that the Risen Christ comes to quicken in the innermost heart of man, we know that there is nothing euphoric about it. It implies a struggle to let all men have part in that same liberating festival.

As a direct result, we shall consider how the Risen Christ is urging us to follow this through to the end: he is preparing us to give our life so that man be no longer victim of man.

'Giving our life', not just a part but the whole of our life, and throughout our existence. Preparing ourselves for this in diverse ways: within oneself, in cells, and by a host of different means . . .

. . . 'so that man be no longer victim of man', whatever be the form of oppression—interior or exterior—that weighs him down. Becoming aware of oppressions. Committing our energies to breaking with situation where man is victim of man. Rejecting privileges. Refusing the hunt for success. Furthering communion between men. Finding liberation—our own, and our neighbour's both near and far away. Being released ourselves so as to secure others' release.

Together, imagining concrete means of living out these realities, with a great multiplicity of expressions and according to each one's various commitments in professional, church, and political life.

In the course of this last year we have discovered that between us we have such a range of diverse aspirations that we are all the more attentive to one point where there is unanimity of faith: our common celebration of the Risen Christ.

In preparing to give our life because of Christ, we are bearers of joyful news to all men, without any segregation whatever. So that all this may pass from one to another, to go out to tell those around us, so that little by little it may bring back to life all that is inert among Christians, we are still situated in the hidden, underground movement of the Church.

We are being led to live incognito, like leaven hidden in the dough, like seed buried in the ground, seeking poverty of heart, always using poor means, without gold or silver.

(*Intercontinental Team, Easter 1971*)

Becoming involved means finding a new way of looking at things; then, instead of being spectators, we become protagonists.

We cannot be satisfied simply with a change in personal relationships; starting from ourselves and inner resources, we must always aim at those changes in structures and systems which our respective situations demand. Only then can we understand the place of personal participation in organized action at professional, trade union, or political level. To discover this, we need the help of competent people and continuous effort to make clear, sound analyses of those local, national, or global situations which ought to be made more human.

The Joyful News strengthens me in my desire to struggle that man be no longer victim of man: this news is for me a real light of hope, piercing the dark places of life in a capitalist society, giving me growing desire and dogged perseverance for this struggle, as if it were a matter of life and death.

*My way of preparing for the Council of Youth in the U.S.A.
is resolving to give up my most precious possession, my life;—
and this for the sake of others, not to gain their gratitude or
my own fulfilment, but simply because it is necessary.*

. . . For me, giving my life today means losing it through
exchanging a very active student life for a contemplative
religious life that is apparently useless and hidden.

I can scarcely understand how to live before God on behalf
of others. The people of whom I am part, who are part of me
to the very fibres of my being: young people, especially at
the university. I know that the same tensions exist within me
as in them; hope and disgust; atheism and living faith; richness
and poverty. . . And my life means being in the Church before
God, convinced that to do wonders and to change the face of
the world. He needs only our radical and unequivocal 'yes'.
It is only when our life is lost to our own eyes that it bears
witness to one who is Other than ourselves and that, somewhere, man ceases, without always knowing how, being
victim of man.

*In the course of a conversation we discussed what our com-
mitment should be, in our family, in our work, in our
university, and in our nation. We talked for a long time
without managing to say anything concrete. But a young
worker brought us back to reality: can we go on just discussing, while men are dying of hunger and because of war;
while men are laying down their lives because they see that
many of their brothers cannot be men? For a moment the
question stumped us.*

*The peace we are asking for is not the kind that dictators
talk about—a deathly silence! But a peace which springs from
justice. We remember Isaiah who says that peace is the fruit
of equity among men, that is to say, the fruit of love, of the
end of exploitation and dependence.*

But how can we become committed to building up this

*peace? Firstly, by watching our own everyday situation with
critical eyes, at individual, local, and national levels, and by
trying to discover what we can change there.*

*We realized the danger that lies in our being satisfied with
our own individual change of heart. We must not forget that
beyond ourselves there is a system and structures which we
must change as well, and that every individual action has a
political dimension.*

*We do know that it is difficult. We think of Argentina and
our return there: will we be capable of continuing the
struggle so that all men can be truly free, and of building a
structure in which it may be possible to love?*

. . . 'Struggle and contemplation': how to avoid making of
them a new dualism which tears us apart, but rather to forge
them into a unity which day after day will push us on
nearer to man? What we are expecting now from the
Council of Youth is to learn from one another how to become
men of communion, who will go ahead and explore new
valleys on the other side of the mountains, and then call the
whole nation to which they belong to a new adventure.

We are always wondering how to find ways of uniting
everybody's efforts for Christ and for man . . . the energies of
many people to wage war on the diabolical spiral of the
capitalization of money by the State or by individuals: a
spiral that stops many Christians from really being Christian
and many men from being free?

HE COMES

Christ comes.
Again and again he comes
walking into our today
challenging us, leading us, loving us
into responding anew to his call.

He ministers.
Who are the oppressed?
Many, but not we
who have received already
the good news.
We know Christ
has broken the barriers
of darkness with light,
of death with new life.
The impossible made possible. . .

Hung on a cross
not to stay,
to return again each time we come
to lay our burdens there
and discover the way
to pick them up again
to go with lightness
forward, reborn.

Christ the challenger
Opening the way for us
to realize what we are
capable of becoming
through him.
Here is the source, the water
from which will flow
the springtime of the Church.

The Easter Christ :
dead and risen,
inviting us to leap
across the barriers into the tomorrow
of the Church :
with doors flung open
a place of sharing all
with all.

He comes
that we might live
to dream with daring,
and pray with hope
for a potency that creates
into reality a decent life
for all men.

Christ
  man
    comes . . .

(Karol, Los Angeles, U.S.A.)

IMAGINATION AND COURAGE

How can we become signs of contradiction according to the Gospel?

We have only two more years in front of us and during them we shall not be afraid to taks risks. Two years is a short time in comparison with the enormous strides which we must accomplish in our common commitment.

These two years will be years of imagination during which we shall search for the precise, concrete form the Council of Youth will have.

They will also be years of courage, during which we shall be trying to hasten towards man's tomorrow, towards a technological civilization with enormous potential for the promotion of the whole of mankind. However, we shall not hesitate, if it is necessary, to become signs of contradiction, when profit and consumer-values become dominant.

As we draw on the Risen Christ as a source, we are invited to create constantly, to bring to re-birth rather than simply to reform. This is the exact opposite of an easy option: nothing is created easily.

Although a desperate lack of confidence in man pervades the present time, we know that 'the Risen Christ will give us enough imagination and courage'.

So for two more years we shall continue our interior adventure, as part of the hidden, underground movement of the Church; what we live may sometimes remain quite secret. We shall continue to use only poor means. Then the world-wide Council of Youth will begin.

(Intercontinental Team, Easter 1972)

'Protest' is so much a current word that we often use it when we want to imply 'contradiction'.

Protest is ultimately negative: a more of less violent 'no', a rejection: protest against systems, authority, society, accepted scales of value. It may be right, but it seems to stop at that.

But on the other hand 'contra-dict' contains 'dictum'— 'saying'. Contradiction is to say 'no', but doing so by proposing another way of living.

So of course it is something costly—are we ready to pay the price of contradicting not just verbally, of course, but through our life, taking risks? And becoming a real sign of contradiction.

There could be a risk of provoking contradiction deliberately, for its own sake: a kind of pointless game that would only nourish some hidden bitterness within ourselves.

So we aspire to become signs of contradiction 'according to the Gospel'. I think that this implies that the fundamental motivation for our living lies beyond simple factors of revolt and inner strife, and is anchored in the Gospel. Of course any sign lived by us will be incomplete, ambiguous, misinterpreted. But it is a sign that finds its true nature by reference to the ultimate sign of contradiction—Christ on the cross.

Many things in the modern world are worth contradicting, and so much of the Gospel merits being proclaimed anew. But the thing is to choose in our own situation, given our abilities and the possibilities open, the direction in which to move. Conscientious objection, help for the Third World, opting out of the affluent society, opening one's house to all comers: four ways among many others; but so important not to think we can live all of them. Else the result is not a sign of contradiction but a sign of indecision as we flutter around.

I know there will be many problems facing me when I go back to my engineering studies. The atmosphere in which we work is cold and 'technical'. In relations with others, it is really hard to get beyond formalities and discover the people behind them. It is difficult, too, to break out of this closed world, not just because there is so little time to spare but because of the spirit and the mentality that are created within it. This is the world of efficiency and security and programmes. In that kind of ethos, how can you live the dimension of gratuitousness, of hope and contemplation, so as to be a sign of contradiction?

Over the last few days, I have been thinking how terrible it is to see the way in which technology is presented as an end in itself, quite detached from human problems. Who will show us how to put soul into this 'netural' world, with its own internal laws?

And when you realize how the role of the technician is growing in importance every day! Perhaps they will be able to set the tone for life tomorrow; but they have not gotten there yet.

In the contruction of the new world, who will help us to keep man constantly in sight?

Sometimes I get scared. Yet at the same time I am aware just how extraordinary the present process is, so full of potential for construction and real advancement.

When I look at the realities that make up my life, I realize that it's not all that wonderful. I would like to create a new style of life and I want to bring about change. Just as Easter is the passing from death to resurrection, the Joyful News is for us the announcement of the possibility of passing from a situation of tension into one of coherence, from oppression to communion, from slavery to liberation, from indifference to awareness, from a naive consciousness to a critical consciousness, from winter to a springtime of the Church, from intolerance to love and from division to reconciliation.

But to live that out, there are risks that have to be taken. It is not easy to make my life into this constant passing from one state or situation to another. My life means my inner life as well as the external situations on which I can bring pressure to bear. The crossing over does not happen painlessly. It is hard and it entails suffering. For it is really a matter of birth and rebirth.

But where does the strength for this rebirth come from? Becoming signs of contradiction in the name of the Gospel

72

means knowing also times of discouragement, yet nevertheless going on, taking one step, and keeping going: taking the second step, and the next and the next as well. But what is the source of our constancy? It is the Risen Christ. He reveals to us our powers of loving, he makes us transparent and makes us in our turn become revealers of the powers of love on the world.

A VAST CONSULTATION

At the point that has been reached, it has become necessary to begin summing up what is being lived in the long march. A vast written consultation is the best means of doing this. We do not yet know what the Council of Youth will be. How can we imagine it? How are countless people whom we do not know living the preparation for the Council?

A questionnaire has been drawn up and sent out to 131 countries where the *Letter from Taizé* is received. Here are the five questions:

1 How, concretely, do you envisage the Council of Youth (for example, ways of working, themes, etc.)?

2 Taking into account the great diversity of countries and situations, what life-style can be imagined, for those wanting to intensify the preparation of the Council of Youth and who are not afraid to become signs of contradiction, according to the Gospel, rather than let themselves be taken over by the system that they live under (money, profit, consumer society, careerism, etc.)?

3 By what means (in solitude, in cells, or in communities) can we become bearers of the festival of the Risen Christ, and how can we transmit this to our societies, with their imbalance of abundance of or poverty?

4 How can we help to find a new face for the Church, allowing it to be the bearer of that liberating festival for men?

5 What really new individual or communal acts of courage can be imagined, so as to continue the struggle in poverty of heart, even going so far as to give one's life so that man be no longer victim of man?

THE FIRST MAIN LINES OF
THE WORLDWIDE COUNCIL OF YOUTH

On Easter Day 1973 there were some 18,000 people at Taizé
to hear Brother Roger give more details about the opening
of the worldwide Council of Youth. He announced:

In 1974 how will the Council of Youth begin? What will
be the first parable on our way forward? One idea has
come from Africa and has been retained:

Amongst other things, the first year of the world-wide
Council of Youth will be one of great mobility, from continent to continent. There will be several successive openings of the Council of Youth, from one continent to another. Next year at Taizé, the opening of the Council of
Youth will take place from 30 August to 2 September 1974.
Then, in the months following, other openings of the world-
wide Council of Youth will take place one after another
in Africa, Latin America, Asia, and North America.

Then an Intercontinental Team set out the first main lines of
the Council:

In our march towards the Council of Youth, through an
intense preparation, one certainty is growing stronger: we
are moving towards an event which will demand more and
more of us, far removed from short-cuts. What will it be?
Already, from the multiple replies received from young
people, three main lines are sure:
— set out as a whole people on the move together
— explore all the dimensions of the people of God
— on our way, create parables and gestures which will be
signs of contradiction according to the Gospel.

I   The fact of having chosen to gather in a worldwide
Council of Youth has prepared us to live an event in
and of the Church. Setting out as a whole people on

the move, we are determined to ensure a radical rebirth of the whole people of God, in order that the Church be consequent with its universal calling, that it become a place of communion for all men, especially attentive to those who are poor, a Church devoid of means of power, in no way compromised with the powers of exploitation.

2   To begin with, the Council of Youth will seek—without fear of the unknown—to explore simultaneously all the dimensions of the people of God:

— *the dimension of depth:* moving from doubt towards belief; this means searching down more and more to a source—the encounter with the Risen Christ.

— *the dimension of breadth:* seeking to inscribe the Gospel within the history of men; so sharing in the struggle of those who are oppressed; uniting ourselves too with those who, without sharing our belief, are bearers with us of a common hope.

— *the dimension of height:* a sense of the gratuitous; revealing to one another the creative capacities hidden within every human being and so working out our search in the beauty of common prayer, in art, and in all the ways by which men express themselves.

3   We shall let our communion spring up and mature in unaccustomed ways:

Always maintaining the interior adventure, as we advance we shall try to create together parables and gestures that speak to our deepest selves and which, better than words, assert our hope. Without any long-term plans decided in advance which would prevent us being free to hear what the Spirit is saying to the Church through the new generations, not following ordinary conference procedures, we shall advance from one provisional stage to another.

— All the time there will be a constant process of summing up the suggestions coming from all the continents.

The same Intercontinental Team also proposed a theme for 1973, the last full year left before the openings of the Council of Youth:

STRUGGLE AND CONTEMPLATION
TO BECOME MEN OF COMMUNION

Before the opening of the world-wide Council of Youth, in this new stage of preparation for it, there remains one intuition to be worked out

'Becoming signs of contradiction according to the Gospel' is leading us to be, at the same time,
TIRELESS SEEKERS OF COMMUNION.
    The communion that we are discovering
    does not mean running from crises and confrontations
    it is always the fruit of pain and labour.

It unites us first and foremost
with the man who is oppressed,
with whom we long to strive
for a liberation that involves us both.
    It is a communion full of new energy:
    crossing, one after another, all the frontiers
    set up by age, culture, race . . .
    until it can reach out to invite all the millions
    of peasants, workers, unemployed, students, migrants . . .
    who in the southern continents especially
    are writing—by their lives—in letters of fire
    the reality we are seeking.
Any seeker of communion
with God and with man
is at once seized by the tension:

STRUGGLE AND CONTEMPLATION
Two attitudes that seemed to contradict or oppose each other,
and finally one is found to lie at the heart of the other,
one begetting the other
in a ceaseless exchange.
STRUGGLE, within ourselves,
to be freed from interior prisons
and from the desire to imprison others;
to throw aside all that breaks our communion.
And struggle in company with the man who is poor,
so that his voice may be heard,
oppressions smashed
so that together we can be re-born
to new relationships of communion.

CONTEMPLATION,
setting out in quest
of a communion with the Risen Christ,
so that the gift of our lives can be rooted there,
and so that little by little
our way of seeing can be transformed
until we consider man and the universe
with the eyes of Christ himself.
Still situated in the underground movement of the Church,
more and more aware that we are not alone in our struggle,
each one borne forward by the other,
this year we are called to work out this intuition:

STRUGGLE AND CONTEMPLATION
TO BECOME MEN AND WOMEN OF COMMUNION.

(Intercontinental Team, Easter 1973)

A sky filled with stars

A TALK WITH BROTHER ROGER
THE PRIOR OF TAIZE

Once a week all the young people at Taizé gather around Brother Roger. He talks about what has gone on that week at Taizé and takes up questions faced by the Church or by contemporary societies. And he always says something about prayer, since it is the core of his own life. Young people are more interested in people than in ideas, and expect answers that are spontaneous, immediate and personal; they want to know how someone lives, and what he is saying . . .

The prospect of the Council of Youth produces in some people an apprehension that is perhaps only fear of youth. Does this ever happen to you when you realize that the Council of Youth is nearing?

With the Council of Youth in mind, we have certainly taken many risks, but I cannot bring myself to worry when people put their finger on the real difficulties. Why? Quite simply because I have confidence in the intuitions of the young people from so many countries who meet here, who go off again, who search, who pray, and who come back again. On certain warm nights, with thousands of young people staying on the hill, I chanced to be out walking alone, under a sky heavy with stars. And I told myself: the multitude of intentions of these young people glimmers like streaks of fire in my night. For the present, there is nothing that can be readily perceived, and yet my night is festival, it is ablaze, heavy with a reckless hope. The future and the young people: they are one. No, I have no fear for the future. A springtime of the Church awaits us. Soon it will warm us with its fire.

Are the intuitions of the young which you speak of so often, easy for you to listen to and to understand?

I am aware that I am a man with limitations; that conviction is deep in me and comes from my whole education So I listen to the young and say to myself: What is happening on this hill where at first you lived alone? You never thought you would see such crowds here, especially not these crowds of young people. A man who is growing old does not expect to see lots of young people in the place he frequents. And now they are coming in ever greater numbers.

I often ask myself: Who are you? And I answer: A poor man who does not know much. Then I ask myself: What are you hoping for? What is your hope for young people? If they loved Christ and if they loved his body, that unique communion called the Church, it would be wonderful. But there is nothing you can do about that. You are a poor man.

You are convinced that many intuitions will come from the young people of the southern continents. Why?

Because through the young of the southern continents we can return to the sources of real humanity. Some Brazilians once said to me: 'We are emotional beings, we are sentimental, nostalgic and incapable of solitude'. We occidentals are people who through our education and our ancestral heritage have acquired control over ourselves. But in so doing we have lost freshness, spontaneity, and the inclination to play. We know only how to earn money. We work in order to earn. We rest to be fresher for work. What a concept of living! With them it is just the opposite. They throw themselves into life and know how to laugh and weep and play. . . . It is they who will give us answers for the ecumenical vocation.

You have announced that the Council of Youth will begin in 1974, but you say also that it will last a long time. Have you yourself any idea of how long that will be?

Certain Africans have told me in their letters that the Council's preparation is hasty. According to them it would have been better to have waited a little longer. And so they hope that the Council of Youth will last as long as possible. That is all we know at the moment.

Are you running into many difficulties during this time of preparation?

With many young people, both here at Taizé and far away, we have tried to turn over the dried-up earth of our lives in order to be able to live this adventure within us. There have been encounters all over the world, with so many discoveries and treasures of mutual trust and friendship.

But of course we have discovered shadows as well. During recent months various ways of resolving certain divisions between Christians were suggested, and the result of these suggestions was a backlash of fear. We here at Taizé were subjected to almost unbearable pressures. And we found that people are afraid of youth, afraid that here we listen too much to youth. I have even been told : 'These young folk will end up leading you on a string!'

But we must forget these rear-guard skirmishes; for then there remains, very strong between us, a searching, a multitude of aspirations, a dynamic force capable of carrying us far, very far.

We must realize also that no great adventure together can be carried out without the appearance of temptations; Christ himself met them. The seducer offered him all the kingdoms of the earth if he would submit to him, the divider. For all of us there are names for those 'kingdoms of the earth'—the attempt, so vain, to gain influence over others, the desire for power. That is most surely real sterility.

Do we know how to watch and pray so as not to enter into temptation? Do we know that at the opposite pole of the free giving of the poor in heart, is the spirit of domination that could even lead to using the Council of Youth for oneself? And that would be devastation, a kind of death.

Death and resurrection! Death and transfiguration! The two realities are part of a single adventure. On the one hand the temptation to make use of others, to use them for one's own ends. And on the other hand the transfiguration of our temptations, of our difficulties, of our refusals. We have nothing to be afraid of in all that, because even our struggle for limpidity of heart becomes a cause for festival.

Who is Christ for you?

He is the One from whom I am living, yet he is also the One for whom I, along with many others, shall always be searching. How many times, with so many people, do we set off again from doubt towards faith : 'I believe, help my unbelief'. And in growing older, faith becomes less arduous, certainty prevails.

Christ for us is the unique source of every commitment for mankind, be it political or otherwise. Were this not so, we should be in danger of using the name of Jesus, after the event, to cover over what has been mere projection of self.

Christ exists for himself. In spite of the silence that may endure within some of us, there is one thing that we can say to him : We believe in you even when you seem to be silent, your poverty inclines us to await and to expect . . . and we are there, poor and vulnerable, searching for him, holding ourselves before him so that he be our basic love and thus, directly, our essential joy.

You have often spoken of a failure in ecumenism . . .

Our responsibility as Christians is the credibility of the Church in the eyes of those who cannot believe. On the eve of his death, Christ set a fire in the conscience of the Church. He prayed : May they be in communion with one another as I am in communion with the Father, may they be one so that men may believe. For Christ our visible communion is not to be cosy together, or to be more powerful, it is to make the Christian community credible for others.

The ecumenicity, the catholicity of the Church, is fire. Yes, that man may believe the Church, it is essential that our communion should become once again visible to all. For the Church is not an end in itself, but exists for mankind.

Now many people today see that after making real head-
way, ecumenism is bogged down in interdenominational institutions that reinforce and maintain parallelism between
separated Christians. These institutions are therefore likely to
prevent the achievement of real communion. Because of these
hindrances many of those who had placed so much hope in
ecumenism now employ their energies elsewhere.

Young people themselves don't even give it a thought any-
more. As for me, on days when I am even faced with attitudes
that are intolerant, I like to think of John XXIII when he said :
'Be joyful, look for the best, and let the sparrows chirp'. The
simplicity of his heart is like a gust of fresh air.

Do you see ways of doing something about this failure?

How can we get out of this impasse so that the Church can
carry out its ecumenical vocation, which is to be a reality of
catholicity and of universal communion for all, where even
the non-believer will be at ease and under no kind of pressure?

Our visible unity implies grounds of unanimity, sources in
common to return to constantly. Can ecumenism lead somewhere without recourse to a pastoral ministry of unanimity,
on a world-wide scale, and this very concretely, because we
are human beings with ears to hear and eyes to see? For me,
a man named John lead me along this path and influenced me
very deeply. By his ministry Pope John XXIII opened my eyes
to a new way of ecumenicity.

Is this universal pastor, the Bishop of Rome, leading us on
towards a Church of communion, one which will not depend
on economic or political power? What are we asking of this
pastor called to be poor? Surely to help us to make read to
each new generation the sources of faith; to stimulate communion between all the local churches and also in a few
words to call not only Christians but also many who listen,
to fight against oppression. And what do we expect of his
local Church, 'this pilgrim Church that is at Rome'? Surely

to warm us by a flame, to stimulate communion between all the Churches.

Now to bring about unity we are faced with this question: will we be able to find a possibility for our present generation, as it stands at a turning point to have, as a provisional measure, a double allegiance? Without asking anyone to repudiate the faith his ancestors have passed on to him in all sincerity, will we have enough imagination and courage to rebuild the unity of the Church, so that we can become a leaven of communion and of peace for the whole community of man throuhgout all the inhabited world?

You speak of a Pope who is poor. It is true that many people reject the institutions of the Church, reproaching them for their wealth. And this in all the countries of the world.

Personally, because of my responsibility as Prior of Taizé, I am haunted by a search: to live Christ for men, with men in order to make the earth a place to live in. Haunted by the need to redistribute the earth's goods among all men; haunted by the injustice produced by the new privileged classes in socialist countries as much as by the oligarchies of countries that are under a free economy; haunted by the power of police states.

I ask myself: Are we men of the Church promoters of justice? Or do we prefer to keep silent when for centuries, not only in society but even in all the Churches themselves, a process has been carried on that creates injustice?

In this domain, the long history of Christians is filled with notorious inconsistencies. Far from living the 'socialization' that was a reality in the early Church, Christians have accumulated possessions. From the sixteenth century on they have accepted a system of work so organized that profit is not shared by all but is kept back for a minority. Did we need the prodding of Marxism to rouse us from our lethargy and to awaken the Church to a springtime by urging it to become a community of sharing, devoid of the means of power, and closely bound to the oppressed?

But at the same time I say to myself: When confronted with the use of money by the Church, to be living stones of that Church is certainly not to condemn other Christians, but rather to search with them; and if need be to come running from the ends of the earth to exhort, persuade, beseech, and to put everything in motion without breaking the communion . . . even if I have to weep alone when I find myself politely listened to, but seeing no action at all. When a man withdraws to the outside to judge, he empties himself of a creative force and loses something of his humanity. But to follow Christ we must be human beings first of all, we must be human-hearted.

More than five hundred years before Christ a man of faith prayed: 'Two things I ask of thee; do not withhold them from me before I die. Put fraud and lying far from me; give me neither poverty nor wealth, provide me only with the food I need. If I have too much, I shall deny thee and say, Who is the Lord? If I am reduced to poverty, I shall steal and blacken the name of my God (Proverbs 30.7–9).

The food I need. Yes, my share of bread, because God does not ask of us a poverty lived in puritan austerity; but not wealth either. Even five centuries before Christ this believer knew that if he had the security of accumulated wealth, he would then only doubt God and say: the Lord does not exist.

What have you learned from your contact with the tens of thousands of young people who camp along the hill at Taizé? Do you feel that you are exactly the same man as before?

I have been through hard stages, through deserts. . . . It is these experiences that make it possible for one to welcome every experience. One evening this year I was surprised to find myself writing in my diary: 'My day has been round'. A round day is a day in which everything in us has been full of mercy. And little by little as one grows older it is the whole of life that becomes as it were round. The advancing years rejoin the years of our youth and there is no break. It is like a sphere in which everything lives and is bound together.

One wonders sometimes whether the young are not happier than their elders. It is hard to know. Personally, I think that Christian education as it was given to us does not promote happiness in living one's youth. The round time comes later on and is only acquired by growing older. It involves finding oneself, freeing oneself of a narrow morality and of mental conformities; then one can rejoice at living.

One loves life whilst growing familiar with the idea of one's death. There is an icon of the Virgin facing my bed. I like to put a light before it at the end of the day and to pray for those who are dying. I cannot bear the death of those I love. Everyone has specific anxieties; with me it is the death of those I love.

What do you think of the current political awareness of many young Christians?

All around us are bands of iron. The increasing search for material security means that around the consumer societies of the Northern Hemisphere more and more barriers are springing up. Every day these societies are becoming richer; we are moving towards a growing imbalance—the overwhelmingly rich northern continents developing an economic system designed to keep the southern continents in a state of dependence.

The more generous-hearted among the younger age-group are appalled to see the inadmissible privileges reserved for just one section of mankind. In the southern continents, this leads the most conscious among them to reject brutally any relationship with the northern continents. In the Northern Hemisphere, we see how children—offered comfort by their parents—are only angered by it; they wear themselves out without actually getting anywhere.

At the present moment, we can see how to refuse any commitment in favour of mankind 'because Christ is all that matters' is to fall into quietism.

How could we say 'Lord, Lord' and yet not do anything to fulfil the will of God? And in that will is concern for man, victim of man. During the Second World War in Europe there were many Christians who prayed, but who remained unconcerned by all that was happening around them—in the extermination camps particularly.

Today, as in the past, our refusing to take any risks, our silences can be a way, whether we realize it or not, of supporting particular political regimes. In certain cases the Churches have been so silent that it has seemed like a clear political alliance, even giving support to oppressive systems. In all this we have to digest our past histories and that is far from being achieved.

And on the other hand, there are Christians reacting against pietism or against the Churches' silences who are ready to take up the most extremist political standpoints and then, having done so, paste the name of Jesus over them as a justification. That could also perhaps be a way of enslaving Christ.

The Christian cannot put the cart before the horse in this way. How to commit one's whole existence to a struggle in company with those who are victims of oppression, with the real risk of losing one's life for love, if one does not constantly draw on the sources of christian life and find refreshment there? Because then man, like God, becomes creative. Involved in an inner adventure with the risen Christ he is part of the progress of mankind, involved as he is at the same time in a fierce struggle for greater justice, towards liberation from oppression.

Struggle and contemplation, Just recently a young Italian Catholic, a trade-union worker in the metal works of Milan with whom I have shared thoughts for several years, said to me, 'The demands of the political commitment of a Christian can be carried out only between the two poles of struggle and contemplation'. Struggle and contemplation—the constant battle of one Italian trade-union worker, and also my own, and yours.

What do you mean by 'drawing on Christian sources'?

Seeing so many young people in the church at Taizé, I never

tire of thinking: what are we all searching for, together? Certainly not some projection of our inner desires, nor some kind of routine. But a way of living intensely—of living a creation with Christ; that reaching down to the sources, praying.

Who would claim to know how to pray? But Christ 'helps us in our weakness'. In what underlies our human make-up—that whole universe somehow beyond our consciousness—he prays within us more than we imagine, more than in any explicit prayer expressed in words. The essential in praying takes place chiefly in great silence . . . and one day, later on, comes the realization that a change has occurred.

Praying without any idea of usefulness, but so as to create, as free persons, a communion with Christ. That happiness, proper to free men, overflows towards others. It is the source of all our struggling—for every man, together with every man.

Many ask how to follow up the search process once the meeting at Taizé is over. What do you reply?

It is not possible to grasp the Gospel in its entirety. But if, during your stay here, you have understood one single word, one single gesture, however small it may be, then live that word, that gesture, straight away and as intensely as you can. Once the first step has been made, this is what will open the way to the steps that follow.

To live the little that we have understood; using that minute intuition as a creative starting point is already a great deal. That means never giving up the struggle: struggle to find an intuition, and to live from it, the struggle to watch and pray with Christ. In the struggle of his agony in Gethsemane, Christ found his disciples asleep and said to them: 'So, you could not watch with me one hour? Watch and pray that you may not enter into temptation'. For ourselves, when we are unable to pray, at least let us watch, holding ourselves present, in silence. Once you have found an intuition, do not monopolize it for yourself. When we try too hard to store the good grain within us, it ends up by going bad. Search for means of communicating it. While not forgetting the hidden nature of the preparation of the Council of Youth, how can you communicate a word, a gesture, where you are, at work, at school, in a café, in church?

Do not try to live the intuition which you perhaps found here in exactly the same way as in Taizé. If you do, you will be in danger of caricaturing it. Try, rather, to be creative from your own starting point: the starting point of the poverty that exists in each one of us. Taizé is only the name of one small family. It is better not to use the name of Taizé too much. Of course one cannot be completely silent about the name of a family which perhaps you love. That would be inhuman. But talk about it as little as possible. Speak rather about the content, about the news proclaimed and lived through the Council of Youth that is in preparation.

A struggle:
To create a communion

PUTTING INTO PRACTICE
WHAT WE HAVE UNDERSTOOD—
NO MATTER HOW SMALL IT SEEMS

Each of us, entering on the preparation of the world-wide Council of Youth, finds himself having to come to grips with the ordinary things of our everyday life, whatever they may be. For example, it is true for many people that one important side of life is their involvement in some political group or trade union. Thus someone has written : *I have discovered a way of living out what the Joyful News says about refusing privileges 'so that man be no longer victim of man' right here in my home situation. Because at the moment we are involved in a revision of the terms of the labour agreement covering our particular category—and it is a hard struggle. . . . As Christians, it is an opportunity to give a real witness of our concern for brotherhood in so far as we can bring ourselves to struggle on behalf of others and not just for our own personal profit. . . .*

Another person has written : *You can find out for yourself the things that statistics do not tell you, that the papers never point out—the obvious wrongs that exist round about you, those that you are guilty of, those that happen close to you. Really listen to what poor people say—the people that no one speaks up for, the ones who don't even realize that they are being unjustly treated. Because only then will we really be entitled to denounce convincingly all the wrongs that exist on a world-wide level—one people oppressing another, one whole class exploiting another . . .*

So it is a matter of really practising the little that we have understood—and another way of saying that is to talk of an intuition that provokes us to create : a struggle to create a communion.

A communion : that means the end of the superficial attitudes by which we avoid or skip around real confrontations :

communion is always the fruit of a struggle, both within our-selves and around us. Finding a way through tensions towards a profound reconciliation—with ourselves, with other people, with God . . .

And it is such a communion that we discover in preparing the Council of Youth. One of the young people writes : *What has kept me going all the time is the thought of how many thousands we are, all over the world, and all struggling, believing, hoping. And because of all the others it becomes possible to hold firm, because of them and also with them . . .*

This communion binds together all who are preparing for the Council of Youth but it is not restricted to them. So many situations, so many forms. Sometimes it involves creating deeper links with others involved around us in a common struggle. At other times it can be a real help to come together into some kind of cell. Or it can mean going to visit each other—as the early Christians did—because otherwise the gulfs dividing country from country, continent from con-tinent will only grow deeper.

A cell—the word is ambiguous. A cell of communion, as the unit of life in a living organism is a living cell. Each cell in the body has its role. A cell comes into being with the discovery that 'we really need each other'. It grows, evolves, deepens what its members live together. It is ready to split or to cease according to the needs of the present moment.

And a communion also means refusing the separations caused by differing ages—no segregation, whether it involves adults, old people, or children.

A communion then that is the opposite of settling down into a closed circle of relationships—that sends such a circle flying in all directions. That is the way that as we advance we have foretastes of the 'Church, a place of visible com-munion for all men'.

So what follows are glimpses into this underground reality : by means of letters, poems, travel-notes, stories of encounters and of things people have lived . . .

THERE IS SOMETHING
NOT RIGHT IN AFRICA

From DOUALA, (Cameroons): *Dieudonné! Quite frankly, we spent a lot of time with him just laughing! With Dieudonné it is so simple. His face, his hands, his expression—they convey something of his home village, his ancestors, all the young people he has encountered on his cross-country journeys . . . He is our gateway to a whole new dimension.*

Dieudonné, what do you find most important in the preparation of the Council of Youth?

First of all, the discovery of a new openness—for example, opening myself to the world and not just my clan. It makes me discover the Protestants and and Muslims living around me. It is so important to understand each other—it is almost all there is.

Unless you are penetrated by suffering you cannot understand other peoples' suffering. The printing workshop, the factory, the pharmacy, and the driving school have meant that I know the suffering involved in working and also the suffering of not having a job. So I can understand someone else in the same situation—someone sacked without reason or unable to find work.

I know that people in Europe also work in the sweat of their brow. I know that there women have to cook for themselves, look after their husbands and their children, and often go out to work as well. But in Africa life is easy for the Europeans; they have a servant and all the rest. And the Africans want the same, even if they do not have sufficient means.

With so many divisions within one country, there are two separate worlds. So it is impossible to know how Europeans really live.

And so many people say, even in the Church, that they have a secret that makes them powerful. But certain Europeans that I have managed to come near to have taught me by their way of living, simplicity, responsibility, their way of using money . . . But there are other Europeans that you only see as you leave the church after mass, whose life you do not know.

So the preparation of the Council of Youth helps us to be ourselves, living our lives with what is at our disposal, and sharing with others. When the starting point is the actual life of each individual, it is obvious that you cannot ask somebody else—Europeans, for example—to solve our problems. But we can share our worries.

There is something sick in Africa: people trust Europeans but not other Africans. The African is told that he does not know how to think—and he believes it. If you are always being told 'You are no good, you are just incapable of anything', you are not going to accomplish anything. So that you have to struggle against this type of exploitation that comes through ideas, radio and television. The people who are educated use their culture to make the rest believe that what they are doing is right and that it is only reasonable for them to be privileged.

How, for you, should the preparation of the Council of Youth be lived in Africa?

Whenever I get asked 'Do you think it is possible to prepare the Council of Youth in Africa?' I feel quite ill at ease because it seems as though the Council of Youth is being regarded then as somebody's property: we can lend it like a suit of clothes. But that means that it has nothing to do with living. To my way of thinking, the real question is 'How can we share, in Africa, with the people around us, all the wealth that we have accumulated within ourselves?' And I know that when it comes down to the way life happens, it is very hard to find answers to that. We find, when we come back to our day-to-day lives, that it is difficult—there are so many things that get in the way. But if we start to look at all the efforts, of real worth, that are being made—in politics, social action, youth groups, tiny cells—then we see that although the barriers are solid, if we look for ways of reconciling our scattered efforts then one day they collapse.

Perhaps some people are living the Gospel without knowing it; we must make it clear to them. If only such people could grasp that they are capable of living by the Gospel—that in their daily living that is what they are already doing—then a lot could change in the Church.

But how do you do that?

There are no rules, no recipes. It needs people who are ready to be attentive, sharing in the same life (not necessarily doing all the same things), who could help others find a sense to their existence in relationship with their actual lives.

Is it better for these 'revealers' to be Africans in Africa?

No, not better! I know Europeans who have done just that. It means overcoming obstacles. It is enough to understand one another. Understanding is done with the heart.

Getting down to the heart: because if you try to understand with the head, you only see general rules. But our heart is great enough to really understand. And if the heart understands, there is no need to ask thousands of questions.

It is the same in the divisions between tribes. A man is suffering: he is the same as you are. Why leave him suffering? But if you look with your head, you see the colour of his skin, where he comes from . . . and while you see the problem, you are not going to do anything. But by using your heart you can both understand him and help him.

Unless you have experienced dying to yourself in your life, if there is nothing broken, then beauty and festival may well be nothing more than a flash in the pan.

How in practice do people prepare for the Council of Youth in the Cameroons?

Well, a lot of thought is on 'man victim of man'. Last Easter's international meeting was mainly about that. The November before, in order to prepare for Easter, we had spent time thinking with some young people about their suffering. And the main points were: social injustice, absence of sharing, man being exploited by his fellow man in so many situations, at every level of life.

And we realized that the main point, the situation that was always present for each one, was tribalism. For example, there is a state of tribalism in the Church: there is one Catholic parish for the Bassa, another for the Bamileke, another for the Ewondo . . . and the same thing with the Protestants. Or else, if a parish has a white minister, that parish goes ahead because he is helped by his community in Europe—he has a car and everything. But if the minister is African, he has only a bicycle, he cannot solve all the problems of each day rapidly and simply. That state of superiority engenders jealousy.

On the market place, why are the prices for Europeans systematically higher? It is not right! But of course, a European's salary is four times that of an African. Europeans really are rich in Africa. It is important to look for the real causes of this state of things; before you can treat a disease you must know the real cause of it.

So for Easter we prepared questions to help everyone think:
—What are our ways of thinking and of acting, what are our attitudes that manifest our racism and tribalism?
—In every stranger we meet, whoever he is, there are values and ideas; how can we find out what they are?
—What has Christ, who at Easter rose from the dead, changed about racism and tribalism?
—What can we do, as Christians and as cells in the preparation for the Council of Youth, to fight here and now against racism and tribalism?

How do you see your own role at Douala in the preparation for the Council of Youth?

As regards the state of youth and adults in Africa, I am in between. Both sides trust me. When I speak, adults listen;

yet young people and I understand each other. So it is important to take advantage of this situation to be a bridge, to explain in both directions what is happening on the other shore. Bringing the young people to the adults, and the adults to the young people: Getting in touch with old and young to see how we are going to live together the Joyful News in Africa.

A EUROPEAN IN EAST AFRICA

We met a very lively group who were writing plays to be filmed and used in school discussion groups. They had been thoroughly aroused by a weekend when they were taken to Mathari Valley, where 61000 people (one tenth of the population of Nairobi) live in shacks made out of newspaper and cardboard, pieces of metal, and anything they can find. There are forty more areas in Nairobi like this and you can find old women sitting on a little pile of belongings waiting for dusk, when they build a kind of shelter for the family before it has to come down at dawn the next day. From this kind of place they were taken to the Hilton, where the manager gave them a guided tour of the luxurious rooms with private showers, the swimming pool, the roof garden restaurant . . . *How can we ever get other students to experience this?* they asked. *There are so many different milieux here; There are the 'wabenzi' who won't make friends with anyone at school unless they first ask 'does your father have a Mercedes?'; they don't even know Mathari Valley exists! And we as students are in such an élite position, how can we ever meet with those working in offices or factories? This is where 'reconciliation' is needed for us.*

I stayed for some time in a fairly middle-class estate (I was surprised when a European who gave me a lift one day said, 'My goodness, that's a bit grim living there, isn't it?'). It was just like any housing estate in any city, though certainly the children tended to stare at first; perhaps because there were only two or three Europeans there, or because I didn't have a car. My first impression of this place was of high walls and a feeling of being completely boxed in! All was of white concrete, with box-like gardens hemmed in by concrete walls about two metres high. People could be heard through the walls, but not seen! So usually the children played on the wide open grass spaces or in the road instead of in their gardens. Sometimes they just came into the house to sit with us; always very curious. Soon the children stopped staring and greeted me. Most parents, both husband and wife, went out to work and during the daytime in the school holidays the estate resounded with children's voices and cries.

This was such a contrast to the 'Jericho' area. From the centre of the city going through a maze of little streets with mainly Indian shops, one comes to a large mosque with white domes and minarets shining in the sun. *Allah alone is to be worshipped*, is written in English in tall stone letters above the doorway . . . but this is in the heart of hectic down-town Nairobi . . . traffic screams round and roundabout and chokes the air with fumes . . . buses lurch along packed so full that people hang on around the doorway . . . pavements overflow with people and market-stalls selling bright material, coloured underwear, scarves, baskets, pots and pans . . . and somewhere in a gangway someone is having his hair cut sitting on a chair, with a piece of mirror propped up against a tree. . . on we go down the road leading to 'Jerusalem and Jericho'. *There's a huge new church with a tall tower at the corner of the road . . . you can't miss it;* we found this so true: it stands out a mile above all the tiny overcrowded houses packed like little boxes all around . . .

Some we met felt it was so important that their image of Europeans should begin to change, but also that the tourists should not build up an image of Africa just as one vast game reserve with a few strange tribes. *What can you do when you get back to England to change the image people have of us over there?* This was a question we were quite often asked. HOW can one *listen* enough to people when one is in their country to begin to understand and not just to react to superficial things? And then HOW to give a balanced image to people at home?

What do people think of Europeans and Europe?

'Mzungu', a common word for European; in Swahili this comes from a root meaning 'cunning, crafty'. This concept comes in some African literature: discussing this in a school in Tanzania, a student said they used to think Europeans had such superior knowledge that they could even read one's thoughts (especially those of people with piercing blue eyes!).

Many examples were encountered of thinking that ALL Europeans must be RICH. Even if a European lives in a poor way in Africa he is suspected of having a big salary paid into his bank at home—sometimes this is true . . . sometimes it is certainly not.

Often both Africans and Asians are surprised that a European woman can cook, sew, do housework, iron, etc., etc. These things actually are remarked on! A group of seminarians in Kenya said, 'We only see Europeans as administrators, teachers, wealthy farmers . . . we have rarely seen "ordinary" people and have rarely met them to share ideas'.

Sometimes Europeans are thought of as unfriendly because of different customs . . . an African will always stop and greet people he meets along the road. Hospitality . . . an African will just go to someone's home as a sign of friendship whereas a European will wait for an invitation . . . while the African wonders 'why doesn't he want to come and see me?' . . . If an African offers food (which he will do at whatever time of day one visits him) then the visitor will share with him. But sometimes a European will say that he has just eaten—this is then interpreted as 'Why does he refuse to eat with me? He must think I am too inferior to share a meal with him'.

A European can often feel that Africans put him on a pedestal. Often it is difficult for an African to think that a European will be ready to share and live in his home; at a conference in Kenya students couldn't believe that a European could sleep in the same dormitory with them and eat the same food; they asked, *Has one of your ancestors been an African, that you can do this?*

What were the reactions to the Council of Youth?

Sometimes people found themselves already involved in the preparation . . .

104

'Ah, that's just what I've been waiting for . . .'

'We are already involved through sharing with you; what can we do next?'

'Don't lose that message . . . it's so important . . . especially that we must look at the little that we have and work to use that more fully . . . we so often miss opportunities because we cry out that we haven't enough money . . .'

'I only begin to see how important it is now that you are leaving . . . I wish I had made more time to meet you . . .'

In Tanzania many are already searching for a 'new face' for the Church, and so find themselves immediately linked . . .

'We need to arrange a meeting here, in Kenya, so that others can experience this . . . we have tents for 100 people . . . why not hold a meeting here?'

'I like the message . . . it's very sensitive . . . do they think of the Risen Christ in times of crisis? We need to live this rather than discuss about it . . .'

'It helps me to see that there are people in other countries who are questioning like me . . .'

Some reactions against . . .

Why can't you follow these themes without linking it with religion? (attitude in Uganda and Tanzania)

Fear that it might be too political . . .

In Uganda some thought we needed to have a Council of Elders, not a Council of Youth, because there were many examples of young people not being allowed to be heard when they voiced an opinion (it's a great taboo for young people to express an opinion, either in a meeting or at home . . . only those who reach the status of 'elder' in church or tribe can join decision-making discussions).

Quite often we were expected to give a 'follow-up' scheme of discussion or work, and it was very difficult to stimulate their own inspiration.

In Kenya they expected something highly organized and committees etc., because of well organized conferences there and quite often too much bureaucracy.

We talked to a priest as he took us back into Nairobi . . . and we began to see him as a man who is really prepared to take *risks* so that there is the possibility of *growth*. He told us: *Really to LISTEN to people here isn't easy . . . it takes lots of time and patience . . . yes, real patience . . . and you have to be able to* risk *everything . . . to leave your own concepts and begin all over again . . . to be prepared to admit that in this culture you know* nothing *and to start from there . . .'*

Again and again I remember what this priest said about listening . . . and I constantly ask myself the question: HOW can one really listen? It's easier to reflect afterwards than to live with more silence at the centre of your life so that you can live this listening instead of merely reacting. I think also of Andrew who said that we often live a reflected life like a mirror, reacting for or against something someone says or does, instead of creating love and living from a genuine centre.

For me, when I left for East Africa this time, I think the most important aim was to listen creatively and in depth, so that through this listening a reconciliation and a sharing might be possible. But can such listening really be done unless one works with people and lives with them for some time?

One kind of listening is to soak up impressions and get the feel of the place . . . one can walk through the streets of Nairobi and see the different milieux . . . but is this enough?

Perhaps in this kind of listening one can begin a reciprocity, a creativity, if one also asks sensitive questions: not ones that are really only a form of 'judging by a European yardstick' and often only provoke reaction; but by asking something which makes someone think further; to begin a dialogue that is creative. Perhaps it is as easy to listen passively as it is to react violently, but how can one develop the capacity to listen creatively?

Sometimes this emphasis on listening can seem to be another form of paternalism! (Especially if you say in a group meeting that one of your aims is to listen!) The reaction often is 'what do they want to find out?' and sometimes in a country where the political situation is not very stable this can cause suspicion. One group we met several times found it quite difficult at first to think about any possibility of sharing ideas with youth of other countries; and it even seemed slightly odd to them that Europeans should want to listen to the values of Africa. Their first reaction was, *Well I suppose we just shouldn't expect to receive so much money in aid from overseas without giving something in return . . . you are asking us to give you something now in repayment?* Gradually as we talked about aid and the image this gives us in Europe of the starving Third World that we should feel guilty about and of the the possibility of a more equal sharing of values, slowly we began to listen to each other and to see some of the concepts that needed to be changed . . . and that images need to be broken through on both sides. This last point seems very important at the moment since there is almost a danger that in leaning over backwards to listen to traditional African culture, one may be trying to revive a 'lost paradise' that in reality wasn't a 'paradise', and this can be paternalism as well! Some people see very strongly that one ought not to Africanize for the sake of Africanization, but that a synthesis is far more true to the situation. Perhaps it is better to think in terms of sharing and searching together instead of 'listening'?

One missionary told us that we couldn't know or begin to understand and share the intuitions in Africa until we had learned an African language. Certainly if English is the only language of communication, it means you can only contact and share ideas with the élite student groups in Kenya and Uganda, and this is even more true today in Tanzania where Swahili is becoming the language medium in place of English. There are also many thought patterns and concepts that are revealed once one begins to learn, say, Swahili. There is one very simple word which is very difficult to translate, but which I find very beautiful, and often feel I want to use it here. . . . I suppose it can best be explained as an expression of compassion, of 'I-feel-that-with-you'.

WORDS

Words, words, words,
Words, words, words
Can I listen past your words
And hear the song you're singing to me?

It seems like we've been talking for so many years
But I haven't heard a single thing you've said :
Is it that we don't quite know just how we want to say it
Or that we aren't sure what we want to say?
Words, words, words . . .

Sometimes I'm not sure quite what your words can really do.
Do they make a bridge between us or a wall?
I've got to find the spaces that are left between your words
And look in there for what you really are.
Words, words, words . . .

I wish that there were some way to tell what you really mean
From the rest of what you merely say :
Perhaps if we could stop a while and listen quietly
We'd hear so much of what we couldn't say . . .

(Kathy, U.S.A.)

FROM HELSINKI TO LOS ANGELES

People trying to live the preparation of the Council of Youth do so in the context of their daily life. For many, it is something that is real, even though they may be quite alone. They try to be a presence of communion for others, in their home or at work. *Here I am, completely immersed in work. Every day something—a conversation, a glance, an event—is a call to which I have to respond. I am very aware that I really need the support of a cell so that others can help me go on. But so far I have not found any others who feel the same need to share in depth. So while waiting, I continue to search for Christ. Many of us live the preparation of the Council of Youth in this way—very aware of the communion that Christ offers us.*

In many very different contexts, people have found coming together more or les regularly in living cells to be a real source of stimulation. Such cells are composed of a small number of young people—usually less than ten—but often they become a focusing point for a far greater number. They are provisional and, like the cells of a body, they come into being and then may sub-divide or cease to exist. There is certainly no 'standard pattern' to which cells conform—they are of vastly different kinds and forms.

Angelina tells something of how she experienced the birth of a cell in Barcelona (Spain): *I had been coming to Taizé for several years, and bit by bit the desire was growing in me to undertake some really demanding kind of shared life—but I could not see how to put it into effect. Then came Easter 1970; I was at Taizé for that and it was for me a decisive day. Several of them were from Barcelona and on returning home we felt 'It is important to meet up with other young people and share what we have just experienced with them'.*

So, we began meeting regularly, to think about the meaning of the Joyful News for us. The four or five of us, closest together, decided to go on and share more together. So our cell was born. *Five in all, all of us working—some carrying on with studies at the same time. That was very important, it meant not being too intellectual. This cell gave a vital opportunity of sharing what each was seeking for the future. In a climate of mutual trust, each of us was able to grow slowly towards his calling in life. Today the bond between us is still strong, even though we are separated and living in different countries. We know that we can count on each other.*

This living as a cell did not in any sense diminish the commitment that we had in the Church at large. A cell must combine the qualities of communion, service, and openness. Often we used to leave Barcelona to pay visits to various groups of other kinds, to get to know situations different from our own. It is essential to be very open, very free, and yet not be dispersed, having a strong central core. So we varied moments of encounter as a cell with moments of contact with others.

This was a spring-board kind of experience for me. To begin with I found sharing everything, including money, very hard. It was as though nothing was really mine any more. Then I realized how deeply we were being united by this. . . .

HOW TO GO EVEN FURTHER?

From time to time, certain young people are called on to free themselves of their ordinary work and to give all their time to some particular aspect of the preparation of the Council of Youth for a while. Angelina, and Klaus from Stuttgart (Germany), are both in this situation. Both of them have made several journeys recently, visiting cells.

A CELL IS ALWAYS CHANGING

Klaus, although it is easier to understand what a 'cell' can be when you point to the role of the living cells in a plant or a body, it is still rather vague. How can a cell be outward-looking and on-going when it is threatened, as any group is, with becoming an exclusive clique?

I know many cells that people joined because they felt lonely. We often live in huge crowds: there are virtually no opportunities for an authentic, relaxed time to share with other people. And even with 'friends' it is often unusual to be open beyond a certain point. So a cell can be a new dimension, just because people are for once really trying to be together, stimulating one another; to be supported by such a cell can already be a tremendous encouragement.

But a 'support-group' is not a new idea, and I wonder if you can say what is different about cells of the preparation of the Council of Youth?

I think it is essentially the constant desire to go forwards, to go deeper. In the cells that I have seen, there is always a longing to discover what the next step can be towards a deeper form of commitment. The Joyful News of Easter '70 is vital for that. It is always there as a kind of catalyst for new intuitions.

Such a cell cannot be satisfied with being a 'place to know each other better': community that only exists to benefit the people involved in it is doomed.

The question that opens up such new cells is one like 'what is the real centre of the community we are trying to achieve?' or 'when do we really feel that we are living something together, and not simply telling one another things?' I have several times heard cells make the discovery that the only time they really felt together was when they were not obliged to talk. Prayer—in silence, or spontaneously emerging from the reading of a text from the Gospels—has been found to be a unique source of vitality in all these cells.

In one sense the cells are far more intangible than all the other forms of fellowship, be they youth clubs, discussion groups, coffee-bars or whatever. Because the search of the cell lies in depth of living, rather than in doing things.

That makes it sound very detached from ordinary concerns.

The contrary is true. The cell must be a stimulus to action.

You see, an action group sets out to be a group because something needs to be done. Once the goal is reached—and often even before—the group ceases to exist. The goal is the only factor holding the group together. And most action groups only exist for a few hours a week, or less, and have nothing to do with all that each one of the members is involved in for the rest of the time. A cell can underlie some person's involvement in such an action-group, as it underlies and inspires—and questions, sometimes—the way in which others are concerned to live their daily concerns in the Church, at work, in their private lives, in matters of public concern. When people belong to such cells in preparation for the Council of Youth, it is assumed that they have each undertaken serious personal commitments outside the cell. A cell is never a way of withdrawing from things; the parallel with certain 'prayer groups' when prayer becomes a substitute for involvement, serves only to underline the difference.

Can you explain more about what it means to talk of 'preparing for the Council of Youth' in terms of the life of such cells?

Anybody who has heard the news, has felt really challenged by something in it and is trying to let that challenge affect his daily life, is certainly preparing the Council—and of course many are living-out such challenges without as yet having heard about the preparation of the Council of Youth, or the Joyful News. Obviously, the Joyful News, like the other texts deriving from it announced each year at Easter in Taizé, concerns each person's entire life-style, commitments, aspirations . . . but it is so true that real life is shared, there is no break between 'I' and 'we'.

These basic texts are a challenge to be lived-out, using the poor materials that are all that most people's daily life offers. The Joyful News, and how it is being put into practice day after day by each member of the cell, provide the basis on which the cell grows and develops. Nobody can do everything, it is always a question of 'what is possible?'.

*I have heard that you dislike the expression 'founding a cell'—
it certainly makes it sound very institutional. Can you say
how somebody begins a cell?*

As I said, many live something of the Joyful News without
having heard it. Those who have found something in it find
themselves looking out for others whose life is likewise an
attempt to express it. This wanting a community because of
what the joyful News opens towards is the first thing. And
sooner or later I find one or two others with whom I can
really share something of my searching, aspirations, commitment. From that moment on, there exists a community
between us and in that community we can go on searching—
together!

Each person matters in a cell. Each one has something
unique to contribute and since a cell is to do with living something together, no one person, however efficient, or dynamic,
or talented can replace another—because that other also has
something unique. It means discovering, as week follows
week, how we can create a life together that is possible for
each, that gives its full value to what each one brings into the
cell. It is something that is always new and very demanding.
The basis is not linked to particular persons, which explains
why cells ought to be very small—say seven people—and
perfectly ready to change composition. I know many cells
which began to meet after people had been to the summer
meetings at Taizé. The first step was to get to know one
another. The strong sense of community that has often grown
rapidly has led certain cells to tackle particular questions.
Some are exploring how students and working people can be
brought together; others are in touch with immigrants.

It is certain that cells need to take risks at times if they are
to continue. Once a very solid basis has been established, there
are some cells in which a real community of life has evolved
—sharing money, goods, and even a common household for
a while. Those involved in such commitments remain part of
a wider cell and see them as a new step in the preparation of
the Council of Youth. It is interesting that such a step is

almost impossible where people are sharing a house already
for reasons of convenience or simple friendship. These grass-
roots communities grow out of a gradual process by which
people grow freer and mare totally committed. . .

I see a large number of cells increasingly concerned to be
attentive to the questions arising in society and hoping to
work out answers within their own lives to some of them.
They are ready to go to any lengths for that and to refuse
any compromise with considerations of comfort. They want
an answer that can emerge within the context of their society
with all its ambitions, greed for money and power, its consumer basis. And they want to find an answer within the
Church : that is hard when the Church is so weighed-down
with acquired wealth that it is little inclined to be clear and
challenging.

Some questions are really urgent :

—How can those who are not productive be helped to find
  their rightful place in society ?
—How can people free themselves from the yoke of activism
  and productivity ?
—Faced with the law of necessity, how can we live as
  'outlaws' and live the festival in man's fulfilment ?
—How does one retain a creative originality in a 'pre-packed'
  society ?

Here are some concrete solutions :

—Sharing with those who are left out . . . children, old people,
  foreigners.
—Commitment to the Church where patience and boldness
  are kept in balance.
—Being involved in education, universities, party politics, and
  groups of immigrant workers.

A cell is a start, a tiny start, on what we dare to hope will be
the future of human living. Before we can hope, we have to
face the reality that we encounter day by day : so often we

want to live in illusions. The courage coming from the quality of life discovered in a cell helps there. And we begin to ask questions, questions that demand answers—answers that we can begin to find. . .

IN FINLAND, WITH CELLS AND WITHOUT

That is in Germany. But the preparation for the Council of Youth is also alive far above the Arctic Circle. In what follows, Anna-Maja and Taisto write about the things happening in Finland.

Margarita and Alois were the first bearers of the news of the preparation of the Council of Youth to reach Finland: we had the impression of the hard snow suddenly blossoming with bright flowers. With their arrival, the first questions: how can I give my life so that separations fall away—not battered by polemics but abolished by warmth and joy? All our separations . . . between old-style groups and renewal groups, between different political parties, between the prosperous south and the slowly evolving north and east of Finland, between students and workers . . . and all the others.

So often the challenges of today's world are met with reluctance here: why should we strive together? What need is there for any link with young people in other parts of the world? We already have our way of looking at belief, homely and tested. From the very earliest times we Finns, cut off by the Baltic Sea, have baked our own bread, fished our own stream, hunted our own reserve. The typical house is not one in a village, it is one standing all on its own. Why not protect what is our way?

And we are not really very sociable people. But things have changed. We too are capable of learning a new way of living, involving neighbours. And this new diversity must not just be accepted but be welcomed—by it we shall learn to know our own roots better.

Perhaps our former isolation explains why, in preparing for the Council, some people have no real cell to live in. Where cells do exist (Helsinki, Tampere, Lappeenranta, Rova-

niemi, Kokkola, and elsewhere) they are too often similar. But within the cells there is a lively bond between the generations, and they include people from practically all religious backgrounds. For us, preparing the Council of Youth means discovering faces and the people behind them, it means changing the old instinctive reaction of 'I am right, you are wrong'.

Distances here are such that we can rarely be together, therefore prayer and letters form strong links. Here are quotations from some letters:

I am often in contact with Marxist students: their faultless ideology with its very concrete and clear goal is so close to young people's desire for a real commitment and for security. Often in preparing the Council of Youth I am tempted to use the same methods. But then I come across someone in whom my first attitude is to see an 'enemy', a stranger, and I finally realize that the way ahead lies in being without defenses, an obvious poverty—that is my ideology.' *(From Tampere and Rovaniemi)*

Be a sign of contradiction? I cannot as yet presume to such a clear-cut position. People here are so sensitive, so easily hurt. But to be a sign of reconciliation, leaven of unity . . . with each day a gleam of hope, Christ himself. No way now of living without his presence. *(From Kolkontaipale)*

We long to advance. New cells arrive almost every day, new paths to venture along: there are the immigrant Finnish workers living in Sweden that Irja and Eeva visited at Christmas and with whom we now have plans for all sorts of common projects. We are also thinking of ways to help the schooling of children in the very far north of Finland. . .

WAKING UP TO NEW VALUES

Let us go back to the conversation with Angelina, just back from North America where she met groups of young people: *After a month of travelling in eastern Canada, I have the impression that there is a whole deeply-rooted tradition of faith ready to be awakened: the way in which the Canadians welcomed the Joyful News is a clear indication of this. Cells form part of the hidden life of the Church to be a leaven of the Gospel and a sign of contradiction. Silence, service, imagination, prayer are the new values of this simple life and they give a new way of looking at daily reality. One girl was telling me:*

At the hospital where I work, I made the Joyful News come alive as I talked to an older woman. For six years a diagnosis of mental debility had kept her shut away. By taking time to sit and listen to her I was able to discover that it was only a hypothetical diagnosis. People had assumed she was feeble-minded and so finally she became so. A friendly encounter was enough to help this patient to make progress, much to the amazement of the doctors. A whole approach to be re-examined. . .

Another sign of reconciliation: three young people from Quebec (French Canada) living in a small community in Ottawa (English-speaking Canada). One day some young people from Montreal and Chicoutimi went to visit them and found a grass-roots community from Philadelphia (U.S.A.) also there on a visit.

Such visits are necessary to maintain a continuity and to foster a communion from one end of the country to another, and across the frontier.

I met other young people who, after travelling in the United States say that there is a problem of isolation among many young Americans. Many whom they met did not know anyone who was not himself white and American, like themselves.

They described several striking features of the 'long march' in the United States: the words 'poverty' and 'oppression' have scarcely any meaning for many young people. They are conscious of American 'success'.

We have all grown up with the certainty of our power and feel responsible for the whole world. The preparation of the Council of Youth is founded on the recognition of one's weakness and of the need for others. This is very difficult for an American to accept—*as a young American was telling us in New York. He was wondering how to give up this feeling of supremacy without being overcome by guilt complexes at the same time and without shirking responsibility.*

Man is victim of man, victim of 'progress'. We met young people involved in various movements for justice and peace. They all have the same ideal of freedom for man and are well aware that the alienation which the U.S.A. imposes on other countries and the Chicano, Indian, black, and Puerto Rican minorities is closely linked to their alienation resulting from a consumer society.

Another travelling cell of people from Europe and Sri Lanka (Ceylon) spent several months meeting and listening to young people in Hong Kong, Australia, the New Caledonian and Fiji Islands, and New Zealand.

In Hong Kong, after days of intense contact with many people: Christians, non-Christians, communists, and with much sharing and searching—so many problems are being tackled— we suddenly decided to make the fort-five minute bus ride to the Chinese frontier. We were accompanied by two Little Sisters of Jesus—one from Korea, the other from Vietnam. Hong Kong! What a town! 80% of the population is reckoned to be communist. The bus ride is as hectic as usual, past buildings covered in huge red and gold signs that we are told announce new restaurants, or a marriage. We learn something of Vietnam. The sons of a family are traditionally responsible for their parents. The war has prevented many from fulfilling their duty and the result is a breakdown—economically, socially, psychologically. Leaving the bus we walk a few hundred metres, and find ourselves against a rather solemn fence beyond which stretches a delightful shady path: China! Like so many others, we climb a hill and glimpse a little river, fields, some small villages, and a few fishermen who are for us the representatives of 700,000,000 million others. We feel very close and yet very distant and foreign.

In Australia, we were able to have many contacts with Aborigines, either with individuals or in the visits we were allowed to make to 'reserves'. One told us how so often a whole tribe is forced off its home land—where fruit grows and game can be found—and is 'rehoused' on a patch of land without hope of anything ever growing there, often without water for irrigation. Then while the original lands are stripped of the nickel or copper found there, the Aborigines are enclosed by a fence and left to die of famine or despair. Yet here is a man, telling us all these things about his people, who stubbornly refuses to hate. He describes how for him it is as though there were a glass wall between black and white. The wall is economic and political, yet it seems to prevent every kind of relationship. For him this wall has to be attacked from both sides at once and he dreams of people of both kinds searching how to do this.

We were struck by the isolation of Australia, and inside the country there are so many groups without contact—not only the Aborigines and the coloured population, but also the immigrants of Greek or Italian origin are seen as 'not real Australians'. How to break down so many barriers? Even the different Churches seem often to preserve attitudes of rivalry and distrust that astonished us at times. It is frequent to see the parishes in the working-class parts of town close down. People there expect little from the Church. So few Australians travel, or if they do, it is normally to England, North America, or New Zealand. But we found it encouraging that a good number of the young people we met are looking towards Asia, and not simply from a tourist point of view.

When we arrived in an Aborigine reserve, the reaction of the children on seeing that one of us was black. . . ! A hero! 'What are the reserves like in Ceylon?' was a common question. In one reserve we learned something of the differences between the various tribes, all with their own tongue, all with 10,000 years of history. How the Northern tribes, in their dances, have a sense of the artistic, room for improvisation, while in the Centre, perfection lies in exact imitation of a received model for both movements and body-decorations.

We were told, 'No one has tried to learn the language spoken here; the whites wait for us to learn enough English'. But how can there be any real understanding on that basis? If you cannot understand the words used, can you understand the silences between the words?

Aloy had a dream: a meeting between men of every race. Each one brings a precious stone. The white man tries to persuade the others that his is the only really valuable one, that they should all throw theirs away; until one of us from the cell intervenes and explains that every stone has its beauty and its value.

MEDITATION SUR NOTRE MARCHE

Méditation sur notre marche . . . toujours trop courte car il
   faudrait l'enrichir chaque jour :
Nous sommes à nouveau pèlerins sur la route d'Emmaüs.
Nos têtes basses ont ému l'Inconnu de rencontre et il fait route
   avec nous.
Tandis que le jour baisse, nous cherchons à tâtons son visage
   et lui vient parler à nos coeurs, déchiffrant le Livre de la
   Vie, il fait feu de tous nos espoirs décus.
La marche en est plus légere, nous apprenons à tisonner,
   à placer braise contre braise.
Ce soir, si nous l'y invitons, il s'assiéra et nous prendrons tous
   ensemble le repas.
Alors y verront tous ceux qui n'y croyaient plus et l'heure
   viendra de la Reconnaissance. . .
Il rompra les pains de larmes à la table des pauvres et chacun
   recevra sa mesure de manne.
Nous rentrerons à Jérusalem annoncer à haute voix ce qu'en
   chemin il nous disait à l'oreille.
Sans doute y trouverons-nous des frères pour répondre : 'Nous
   aussi, nous l'avons rencontré',
car nous le savons : la bonté de Dieu vient visiter la terre des
   vivants !

(Isabelle, Paris, France)

MEDITATION FOR OUR JOURNEY

Meditation for our journey . . . always too short for each day
it must be given new life : We are once again pilgrims on the
road to Emmaus. Our heads that were bowed, roused as we
meet the Stranger who draws near and comes with us. As

evening comes, we strain to make out his face while he talks to us, to our hearts; in interpreting the Book of Life, he takes our broken hopes and kindles them into fire: the way becomes lighter as, drawing the embers together, we learn to fan the flame. If we invite him this evening, he will sit down and togther we shall share the meal. And then all those who no longer believed will see and the hour of Recognition will come. He will break the bread of tears at the table of the poor and each will receive manna to his fill. We shall return to Jerusalem to proclaim aloud what he has whispered in our ear. And no doubt we shall find brothers there who will reply: 'We too have met him'. For we know: the mercy of God has come to visit the land of the living!

SOME LETTERS

FROM SARDINIA : We are concerned not to let the Council of Youth in Sardinia happen without the participation of the young people from the poorest parts of the island—all the agricultural area, the mountainous part, in the centre, north-east and southeast. Every Sunday, therefore, we want to get in touch with the young people in the most remote villages of Sardinia.

It seems as if we have more than enough to do if we think just about the reality of the Sardinian situation in the preparation of the Council of Youth. And here we must show a little imagination :

The Church in Sardinia : what is preventing it being a living sign of the risen Christ today? Traditions, inherited structures, superstitions, sacramentalism without real evangelization? How can we go beyond this? By small, new communities which are signs of love and contradiction in the very heart of the institutional Church.

So that man may no longer be victim of man : Sardinia, the traditional land of exploitation. Problems of shepherds, emigration, miners, schooling. Imagination to find new ways, to accept to be signs of contradiction : co-operatives, education for the masses, conscientization of the very poor.

The flight of the intellectuals to the mainland and to the big towns on the island. No real local awareness of development exists. The numerous regional attempts that have failed show that the ruling political class have lost contact with concrete reality and have become 'armchair strategists'. Here is an open field for any young graduates who are not too preoccupied with their careers, but who are disposed to work for the liberation of man.

FROM BANGALORE (INDIA): Because of the plentiful labour force, the main feature of the work situation in our country is the exploitation of the working class and the quasi-permanent state of injustice. The picture that comes to me is one of the worker as a cheap lemon which is thrown away when the juice has been squeezed out. Then another is bought.

There is a vast work of conscientization to be done: unless the worker can rediscover his dignity, there will be a complete radicalization of the workers' world which could lead to a bloody revolution. The preparation of the Council of Youth comes as a hope in a desperate situation. At Taizé I found international solidarity for the workers' cause. I have the impression that the Church is waking up. Will it play its true role and be a leaven of our unity? If so, there is hope for India.

FROM MARSEILLES: We are trying to do a survey in the African and North African districts here to get to know peoples' way of life and what form problems take: prostitution, unemployment, literacy, lodging. . . At present, one of us is living near the North African district simply to be there as a friend. In different ways others are moving towards political commitment without it splitting us. Yesterday two of us took part as sympathizers in the Communist Party's elementary school.

FROM INDONESIA: If Christians and Muslims work together, it is primarily because their concerns, rather than their faith, converge. They do not talk about faith between themselves. They were most interested in the Council of Youth. One hesitation about the text of the Joyful News . . . but when we explained that the text serves as a source to challenge everyone to be sincere in his commitment and faith, in a spirit of openness and attentiveness for better understanding, then the Muslims took the point and told us how they were struggling for greater justice. Because of their work they have had several arrests by the police.

FROM ALASKA: I think that from my experience at Taizé and visiting other people preparing the Council of Youth in Italy and Germany, one of the most important things for a person to do is to look around him, to take note of what is happening to the people around and what people are doing to (or for) others.

Here in Alaska, as in many other parts of the world, there are people being oppressed and people being taken advantage of. In our state the native Alaskans (Eskimos, Aleuts, Indians) are presently being treated as the Indians on the American Southwest were treated 90-100 years ago: their culture is being played down, their land taken away, their people getting the 'shaft' (mistreated). Things must be done now to prevent the native Alaskan from winding up as the American Indian did—without land, money or culture in so many cases. . .

To live the Gospel, I feel that we must work with the native peoples. Not from the viewpoint of their being 'the poor natives', but as their being my brother and sister.

The native is not the only Alaskan in need, though. The deaf, the poor, orphans, and the homeless, all are either forgotten or ignored. In order to help, all a person need do is stop and look around and care.

FROM DURHAM (ENGLAND): As a cell, we found last autumn a renewed need and urgency for support and real searching. Several had been to Taizé and returned eager to talk, go farther, and very much challenged; but also we found increased difficulty in expressing ourselves and in 'getting down to brass tacks'. So we decided to have more regular lunch times together in small groups just to come closer to each other. There is a danger of being too cowardly, untrusting— and even Christ can be pushed out of the way. We also feel the need to express our commitment in a more concrete way; certainly some of us are growing towards a more communal life. . .'

And FROM LEEDS, (ENGLAND): after the visit of a small travelling cell: This visit made us look at our situations here and helped us bring ourselves to a point where we have either got to take the risk of committing ourselves further to the cell, or not making that move and perhaps going forward by ourselves in a different direction . . . it's just that we'd better get on with something rather than wasting time in too much analysis and being rather too polite to one another. I think we all feel there is a good deal of potential in the cell which is a good basis to go on from.

CANCAO DAS
CASAS SEM VOZES
AOS EMIGRANTES

A beira dos rios nasceram
aldeias cheias de vida
os rios nao se secaram
e as casas estao vazias.

Semearam-se os casais
pelas quebradas dos montes
os montes nao desabaram
mas nas casa ninguém mora.

Junto da areia das praias
brotaram os povoados
as ondas seguem batendo
e as casas estao fechadas.

Que peste negra ocorreu
nesta terra portuguesa
para que os homens partissem
a viver sob outros céus?

(Pedro, Portugal)

LAMENT OF THE VOICELESS HOUSES FOR THE IMMIGRANTS

On the edge of streams sprang
up villages full of life, the
streams have not dried up, yet
the houses are empty. The
houses swarmed up the hillside, the hills have not fallen
but no one is living in the
houses. Beside the sandy shore
hamlets sprang up, the waves
still murmur but the houses
are closed. What black death
has swept over Portugal to
make men leave to live under
other skies?

IN LATIN AMERICA :
LIBERATION AND COMMUNION

A communion? Then what about people living far away, in different continents? How do you live a communion with them?

Well, on any scale there is one gesture that is essential—that of going to visit somebody. The refusal of segregation leads us out of our own enclosed existence. We want to listen to what others have got to tell us. The very first Christians knew that. They made very dangerous journeys just to keep in touch, to share what each little community was living.

And in the preparation of the Council of Youth?

Ever since the preparation began, tiny cells of young people from various countries have been formed and sent all over the world. People who have agreed to give some of their time— two or three weeks and even whole months or years of their life. Little cells of this kind have been sent from Taizé to every continent.

But what do these travelling cells really achieve?

Their intention is to help in the preparation of the Council of Youth in whatever part of the world they are visiting. That means first of all a great deal of listening, then of searching together with those that they come into contact with. Often their visit stimulates and encourages people and many cells and provisional forms of community living spring up as a result. Sometimes the travelling cells organize meetings, so that many can join in. They travel fast, going from town to town, from group to group, spending a moment with a large number of people.

And who pays for that kind of journey?

Often the people making the journey—from savings or by

working for a time first. Everything in the Council of Youth is done with the minimum of means. Sometimes another cell helps in this because they are concerned to practise a real sharing. But no grants or subsidies: rather, we accept the impossibilities that the lack of funds sometimes imposes. All the preparation is lived on the same basis, everything is entirely self-supporting.

Reciprocity: the word is only of use if real ways of living it can be found. For example, the travelling cells often include members from more than one continent. One cell, Asian and European, recently travelled through much of Oceania, including Australia and New Zealand. Another with two South Americans and a Spaniard has been to visit people in Mexico. And in Africa too there are international teams travelling.

Some people can tell us more about all this: Olga and Nestor, Claire, Linda, Joelle, Sebastiano, Claudio. Their journeys were made about the same time. Nestor and Olga are a young, newly-wed couple from Argentina. They recently returned from a journey in Andalusia, Southern Spain. Claire studied engineering at Nancy (France) and has spent some time with communities of young people in Brazil. The other four spent several months travelling through Venezuela, Peru, Mexico. . .

NESTOR AND OLGA

We spent a month travelling in southern Spain, in Andalusia. We contacted a lot of young people, workers mainly, but students as well. We were struck by the fact that it was the humblest among them, those most on the edge of society, whose commitments were the deepest and most demanding. The Joyful News was both an expression of their lives and a challenge to them. They were thrilled to learn that there were other young people of other cultures, other beliefs who, like them, were following a commitment—demanding for themselves, lived for others, for the Church.

We also discovered in our travels that for a certain number of young people living comfortably, with a degree of security, the Joyful News represented a challenge that not everyone

was ready to take up. In Seville, a girl attending a very ex-
pensive school remarked: 'There is no way for me to live in
that way with my style of life,' and so she rejected the whole
announcement. That made us think. She had certainly realized
that the Joyful News demands a radical change in one's way
of living: a difficult and painful passage from the old man to
the new. Not everyone has the strength to do it, so they turn
their backs. She went on to add: 'Only people with problems
can live like that, or a worker, perhaps, not me in any case.'
Her words helped us to see how the 'news' does not evoke
some theoretical judgement such as 'it's well written, I like it'
or 'it lacks doctrinal vigour' . . . but it rather demands that we
opt for a style of living: either our present one, without
cares, or else that difficult one that we want to risk living.
When presented with the 'news', one can only say: 'That is my
life, or that is not my life'.

In Spain one attitude particularly struck us. Many young
people set an alternative before themselves: to struggle to stop
man being victim of man, or else to belong to the Church. We
have never seen the question like that. On the contrary, we
daily join more with the conviction shared by many other
young Latin Americans: being the Church obliges us to
struggle for man's liberation.

CLAIRE

In Brazil I went to visit several community-groups. I also
spent some time living with a team that has been working
amongst the peasants for the past four years, helping in their
basic education.

These communities helped me discover, beyond a certain
popular religiosity of fatalism and superstition that I found
hard to grasp, a profound faith, so far-reaching that I seemed
to be able to read the Gospel in their lives as in an open
book. . .

I saw how one man with more land than some others gave
one of his fields to another man who was in real need and
helped him to cultivate it. A woman was looking after the
children of one of her neighbours who was even poorer than

herself. Strangers arriving in the village are greeted with open arms, as brothers. The common good is considered more important than that of any one individual.

These people have a quite different culture from ours but I find that they are involved in living in an intense way those values that we in Europe only aspire after: here is that Church of poverty that finds its roots in the people, that has no power but is a real sign of communion. I encountered this same reality on the outskirts of Recife, in parts of the city where Christians live together in cells and attempt to discover little by little just what is involved in their struggle against oppression—and that without fear of what it may cost them. . .

So clearly, the Church of poverty already exists, the Church devoid of all the means of power, in which all is shared with all—a Church that is a visible sign of that communion to which all men are called.

CLAUDIO

We cannot remain indifferent to the work now being undertaken by many people with a view to liberation. So we have to give an echo to the youth of Latin America when today they denounce in clear and hard terms the whole capitalist system. That system is based on a privileged minority, gives rise to an unjust form of society in which the main concern is getting maximum value, the basis being profit and competition. We have to work to build up a socialist form of society, having a real humanity, in which the first concern would be man. It is time 'we realized that true socialism is simply total Christianity, with a real redistribution of goods and equality between all the classes of society' (Words of Maximos IV at the Second Vatican Council).

We have to see that as Christians we are called to be signs of the incarnation of Christ in this world. As we work for the coming of the Kingdom of God, we look for the total liberation that we shall attain there. The dying and rising of Christ leads us to live by faith in a dimension of hope: his law is love. And such love as demands justice at any price. So long as there are oppressors and oppressed, where is justice?

Such journeys mean that we come to know one another. Certainly there is no avoiding all the obvious things which divide us and keep us apart, but yet they reveal a communion. Nestor and Olga have something to say on this:

For several months we have been at Taizé and we have discovered a universal side of things. We so want to live the Church as a reality of communion open to all men. We as South Americans have often tried to think of ways of creating a communion between North and South, between rich countries and poor countries—and particularly, of course, between Latin America and the continents of the Northern Hemisphere. Every day, with every problem, the same question arises and it is not easy to answer, perhaps there is no one answer . . . but we must look for one. We are not interested in abstract ideas, our questions arise from what is real for us: our history is one of subjection and exploitation. And because of that history, European attitudes, exterior scales of reference, are still being applied to our continent. But now there is a process of 'Latin-Americanizing' under way that means we are beginning to construct our own identity. This we do by concentrating on what is really, intimately characteristic. The result is often a refusal of everything coming from outside, from the North especially. Many young people are struggling in this direction at present. We see that Europe has been the source of alienation and subjection—so how to continue without any such importation?

As we accept this situation and commit ourselves to the struggle for liberation, our question is how not to cut ourselves off but to maintain a communion with these other countries.

And looking forward to the Council of Youth, how to live this communion? Or how, more precisely, to live the Council of Youth in Latin America? Here in South America there are many young people living the Joyful News without knowing it—above all those who are simplest, poorest, those who never speak because they are never allowed to speak. We believe that Latin America has much to bring, and particularly by these very poor, very simple people we have mentioned.

Our most valuable contribution—and the most original, too —is to offer the world a sign of hope: hope in man, hope that his struggle is new creation.

CHE JESUS

Me dijeron que volvés a nacer en cada Navidad.
Mira que sos locos¿eh?
¿No ves lo que estamos haciendo?
Cada vez que un empresario explota o engana a un obrero,
y un dirigente gremial vende o traiciona a sus companeros,
cada vez que un profesional lucra con la desgracia de otro ser,
cuando un empleado desprecia a sus hermanos obreros,
o cuando un obrero aspira a ser burgués,
busca su propia ubicacion, no piensa en los demas
y no se siente responsable de la liberacion de todos los
    hombres :
cuando un pueblo esclaviza a otro pueblo,
cuando llevamos la guerra a otras naciones
porque tenemos que sostener
esta podrida civilizacion de consumo que nos hemos in-
    ventado;
cuando no denunciamos la injusticia
ni nos asociamos para luchar contra la explotacion,
el atraso, y las causas que prolijamente impiden
el progreso de los pueblos,
vos querés venir nomas. . .
Yo no sé si con tu gesto testarudo de volver cada Navidad
estas pretendiendo decirnos algo.
Que la revolucion que muchas veces solo declamamos
empieza antes que nada en el corazon de cada uno.
Que no se trata de cambiar solo las estructuras,
sino de hacer posible que el egoismo se cambie por amor.
Que tenemos que dejar de ser lobos
para volver a ser hermanos.
Que no perdamos mucho tiempo en criticar
y nos pongamos seriamente a trabajar
por la conversion individual y por el cambio social
que dé a todos los hombres la posibilidad de conseguir pan,
la cultura, la libertad, la dignidad.

Que vos tenés un mensaje que se llama Evangelio
y tenés una Iglesia que somos nosotros.
Una Iglesia que quiere ser servidora de los hombres.

Si es asi, Jesus,
veni a mi casa en esta Navidad.
Veni a mi patria. Veni al mundo de los hombres.
Y veni antes que nada a mi propio corazon.

(A young Argentinian)

OH JESUS!

They say you come to be born again every Christmas.
Are you crazy, man?
Don't you see what we're doing?
When a boss exploits and cheats a worker,
and a shop-steward sells out on his brothers;
when the professional types get rich on the other people's
    sorrow;
when workers only long to be cosy,
trying to make it without thinking about anyone else,
and certainly not thinking about setting all men free;
when one people enslaves another;
when we declare war on others
because it is important to keep going
this rotten consumer-society we've invented;
when injustice is not denounced
and we do not unite to fight exploitation,
delay and all the rest of what prevents
the advancement of peoples.
And then you go and want to come. . .?
Are you trying to put something across,
with your crazy idea of coming every Christmas?

That the revolution we just shout about
starts first in each one's heart?
That it's not just about changing systems—
but about making it possible for selfishness to become love?
That we have to stop being wolves
and start being brothers?
That we waste too much time criticising,
should get to work hard
for a change of each and of all—
to give every man the possibility of getting bread,
education, freedom, dignity?
That you've got a message—Gospel
and a Church—us?
A Church aching to be a servant of men.

If that's it
then come home to me this time.
Come to my country. Come to the world of men.
And first thing off, come to my heart.

SOME MORE LETTERS

FROM ROME: As soon as I heard the news of the Council of Youth, I sensed that it was to do with the Church: something important to live in and for the Church. So often it seems split and divided, torn by discord and by people refusing to recognize others as belonging to the same family.

Here in Rome the preparation of the Council of Youth inevitably means a strong awareness of the tension of a Church that is divided. . . . So many stone churches and so few Christians who are living stones . . . many communities but so weak a unity in the bond of peace . . . and of course the great problem of the institution, the structure.

How to become active signs of a hope, a conviction that reconciliation is possible, at whatever level?

The preparation of the Council of Youth can become the means by which young people learn, by not just meeting separately, how to leap over the walls that divide. The whole Church, and the whole of mankind with it, has to come to discover the joy of the resurrection.

It is impossible to think of Christ and not think of his Church, and to think of the Church means thinking of Christ's longing to see it purified, and renewed. . . . With that, the way ahead seems to involve a purification of one's own heart first, freedom from prejudices and categorical judgements and the false hope of getting somewhere with others when love is absent. . .

To do that today in our Church demands a new courage. Excommunications and divisions are easy to replace by new exclusions and refusals; it is much harder to struggle for a simple and immediate end to the scandal. We are continuing to work quietly, looking for ways of reconciliation; and we are continuing to suffer with the Church 'in pilgrimage in Rome'. It has, painfully and slowly, to free itself from so much heaviness and oppressive superstructure.

But now we are sure that there is one institution we really

must fight against. It is not really one we often call by the name, but the institution that really weighs on us and the whole Church is the absence of love, the absence of that patient love that believes all things, hopes all things, and drops all selfishness.

FROM THE PHILIPPINES: With the support of a bishop, a co-operative of small plantation owners has been set up. He is very welcoming, and we have been talking with him about the problems of growing sugar-cane. He is trying to be a man of reconciliation, and to his table come workers, bankers, and land owners.

We have been two days in a village with a group of young people who are trying to encourage a community spirit among a group of former sugar-cane workers: by means of a strike, they have managed to make the *hacienderos* give them land to cultivate. They have just arrived. They have to build their house; they also have to plough the land, an undertaking which is new to them since they are only used to cutting sugar-cane. Sitting in the village in the evening, they tell us of their many problems. Life is hard for all. There are some who would rather go back to the plantation, where they are sure of getting their four pesos every evening. Here, they will have to hold on until the first harvest in a few months' time, when things will get better. The question is: will they have the patience?

FROM BERLIN: The preparation for the Council of Youth has opened up a new perspective for me: living the contradiction of my personal commitment in a struggle for and against the Church.

The result is a kind of synthesis, sending one to that point of intimate solitude where festival springs into being: the central nucleus. The contradiction can only be resolved there, making that nucleus into the focus of an inward unification.

Trying to realize this unification of myself, and the search for unity with others, without running away from the real contradictions, has made me see the real sense of the Church.

I picture to myself a Church born anew from many such unifying nuclei. The deeper the unity, the further it leads. And the stronger the tensions resolved, the greater surely the resulting strength.

The fact that we do not as yet know what this coming strength will be like, and that an ever stronger hope is inspiring us, are the things most appealing to me in the preparation for the Council of Youth.

FROM LE MANS (FRANCE): You easily end up by feeling guilty because you are 'a student living in a rich country'. So instead of facing your responsibilities, you find yourself making excuses: 'preparing for a future role as teacher or research-worker in a society that we will then be helping to become more just. . .', just forward-looking escapism. Decisions and choices are put off until tomorrow. Even without talking of possible social, political, or trade-union commitments there is the question of what is really being done in terms of human relationships here in the faculty buildings. How can I live out my commitment here in these surroundings, and not just consume what is offered?

FROM AN AUSTRALIAN IN NEW YORK, AFTER A JOURNEY IN EUROPE: The sense of loneliness and 'cut-off-ness' which I experienced deeply at times in Europe and England and especially here in New York, even though among friends, has made me deeply conscious of the emotional forces that all immigrants and refugee ('alienated') people have to contend with in any place. I feel very penitent about my lack of previous concern and failure to 'get alongside' such people in the Australian community. . . I believe this stems out of fear of making myself open to people, vulnerable in other words. This is the question: How do I become 'open' to other people who are different—and with what spiritual resources do I prepare myself. . .?

I think we need to discover some possibilities of sharing in the experience of life from the southern continents, especially the young Christian's political involvements, etc. My deep intuition is that we don't need knowledge alone but rather deep human contact, communion, sharing . . . some means of breaking open the Australian shut-in emotion and spirituality —a resurrection!

FROM A COUNTRY THAT CANNOT BE NAMED : The struggle to be free, truly free, is hard and long. Many of my friends may be dead by now—with the muffled press no one knows. It is indeed strange and ironic that although we do not meet any more (not allowed) with friends, a closer communion has come to exist among us. We are not aware of everyone's whereabouts—it has become a danger to do so. Yet the old ties have become more precious, and the regret that we really did not exert much effort to know each other before, under pleasant times, comes to nag us to become better neighbours to all people. Isn't this 'living the faith'? We often take people for granted. I catch myself thinking of people I did not care for before. Now I worry about them, aware of their needs and their physical weaknesses. The Church of committed Christians has gone underground. . . Think of us and pray for us.

SO AS TO SHARE LIKE BROTHERS

Margarita, you mainly live and work in Argentina, in Buenos Aires. How did you, a Latin American, come to be involved in the preparation of the Council of Youth?

My first contact with Taizé was during the Second Vatican Associations, and called to be present as a lay auditrix at the Council. There I met Brother Roger who was an observer throughout the Council. Then in 1969 he asked me to come to Taizé to help animate the youth meetings there, as a sign of reciprocity between Latin America and Europe. I am firmly convinced that this reciprocity is vital—not only between the southern and northern continents, but also within a country between different generations, inside every family. It is a matter of achieving a real complementarity—both respecting what each one values most and also building on the conviction that we really need one another. For example, do people in Europe realize that they need the peoples of the southern continents, with all their gifts and capacities, if Europe is to become really free?

Margarita, since 1969 you have devoted most of your time to preparing the Council of Youth, either at Taizé or travelling to visit cells in all sorts of countries. Can you say how you see cells living—thinking especially perhaps of what you recently saw in Paris and Belgium?

Certain things are often felt to be characteristic of cells, and if you ask people why they are in a cell the answers will usually be like 'as an antidote to individualism', 'because we want to pray together', 'so as to share like brothers', 'because of the encouragement it gives to get on and do something for other people. . .'.

Such cells meet—six or seven people in general—at different rhythms—every week, or every other week, or for one weekend a month. And as the months pass, such cells have various stages to get through. For example, there is a tension between living as a group and being open to welcome others. Time shows how a readiness to welcome anyone who comes hinders the growth of the group as such. The reaction is a fear: the fear of turning in on oneself, of forming yet another clan or clique. But the solution seems to lie in what one group has said: 'We feel that one real way of living in poverty is to recognize our limits; we just cannot do everything, welcome everybody. If we have set an objective, as a cell, to help each other become more available in service by drawing on a single common source—our prayer together—then we should get on with it. Our group exists because we need it, not so as to give us some privilege. If we really have to set a limit on the numbers, it will be something to accept simply and realistically'.

Every group seems to find itself confronted, in the early stages, with the question of 'what are we going to do? What will be our activity together?' Then it comes home that the preparation of the Council of Youth is principally about making the Joyful News real in each one's ordinary life, in the context of the communities in which that life is led—at work, in school or university, in the Church, in a neighbourhood. So finally the question is not 'what action should we perform' but in the factory, or the office, or the classroom where I spend most of my time at present, what is involved in 'giving my life in a struggle so that man be no longer victim of man?' Where are we oppressors of other people? And how are we victims? Is my parish a 'community of celebration'? How can I turn my everyday life into the 'celebration of existence' that the Easter hope opens into? How to open a way of reconciliation within my family situation, or among the people I work with?

Because that means the question is not one of 'doing things' but of 'living differently'. Praying with others and sharing with others then become something challenging and strengthening for each individual's searching. So how to really translate the Joyful News in one's ordinary daily life? And as a group, how to become a sort of anticipation of the society and Church that we dream of—without privileges, frontiers, selfishness, not concerned to acquire power and influence? How to be a sign of that and to keep fighting for it with all our might? That struggle means understanding clearly what things are about, it means struggling with other people in an organized way—trade unions, student or professional groups, political parties. The aim is a change in the state of things and in the state of minds: for ourselves and around us; there have to be more justice and brotherhood in men's lives.

In some cells there are people who are not Christians: their different source of inspiration does not make them less part of the searching. And all find in a similar way—be it prayer for some, silence and recollection in a search for inner unity for others—the source of their commitments; for all that is what lies at the heart of the cell's life.

In such ways, many young people are living out the present stage—and it is only a stage—in their preparation for the Council of Youth.

LEIPA

Sinä joka katoit pöydän yläsaliin ympyräksi
kun ulkoa katonrajan aukoista tulvi yö
    ja Juudas lähti
sano, tähän piiriin, ympyräksi
    kuuluvatko kieltäjätkin—he kaikki
kuolemanvaarassa, myöntämisen rajalla
joka hetki polkemassa esille
myöntämisen ihmettä
    myöntämisen lupaustasi Herra!
Pakanaäidit kaikkina aikoina
julkeana hätähuutona jaloissasi
saartorenkaaksi sullotut, ympyräksi—
    kuuluvatko sinuun!
Kuollut jyvä
uusiksi jyviksi kasvanut, rikki jauhettu
    Leipä, murusessakin annatko
itsesi kokonaan?

(*Anna-Maija, Finland*)

BREAD

You that prepare the table in the
Upper Room, while, outside, through the
window, night is falling and Judas goes off,
tell me : those who deny, do they too belong
to this circle? All the men in danger of
death, at the very limits of the 'yes', all
those that, each moment, swagger before
the wonder of the 'yes', the 'yes' of your
promise, Lord! The pagan mothers of each
generation, at your feet like a stifled cry for
help, unmoving, in a ring like a siege
encampment, do they too belong to you?
You, grain of wheat that has died, sprung
forth in new grains, milled and broken;
Bread, do you give yourself, even in a crumb,
yourself, completely?

FROM CELL TO
GRASS-ROOTS COMMUNITY

We began one year ago. Not all of us had been to Taizé, but our searching—like that of so many young people in so many places—coincided with the lines of the preparation of the Council of Youth. We were encouraged by the awareness that lots of other groups like ours are trying to live the Joyful News of the Risen Christ in all kinds of local situations.

To start with we were inclined to go round in circles, or to float, not knowing one another very well and being afraid to drop our masks. Slowly things have changed. Often we have talked over a particular Gospel text, with those of the cell who are non-believers; and I feel that the fact of exchanging in great depth between Christians and non-Christians has enriched us all enormously. They too want every man to be able to have access to 'festival'—meaning for them living in a real fullness.

For all of us, festival goes with struggling for justice: so long as I oppress someone, I cannot live any true festival—and neither can he.

So several of us are envisaging political or trade-union action. Already a number of us are involved in teaching immigrants and their families to read and write.

The situation of these new-comers in our town is impossible to accept: appalling housing conditions—without water or electricity, the children playing among the garbage. The usual wrongs at work: additional hours not paid for, incorrect pay-slips, security regulations not complied with. . . But, worst of all, being rejected, being forced into a ghetto. Nobody makes any attempt to know them better; and fear engenders hatred. Yet without idealizing, we can say how much meeting them has taught us: we were, still are, amazed by their sense of hospitality (so forgotten in our society!). And their readiness to share—having very little, they are ready to pool all.

147

And so we advance, drawing on the source of the Risen Christ. Our little cell is now a 'grass-roots community'. We pray together more often, we share financially and we are looking for ways of helping each other more in life. We find it essential to continue now during the holiday season, when tourism, with its oppulent facade, tries to hide how many are poor.

That is our way of living the Joyful News here. We have no intention of this being an example to copy. But we feel we have begun something together, and in communion with many all over the world.

PROVERBS

There, where a brother has gone before you,
you always find a table prepared.

(*Madagascar*)

Woe to the man who has no friend
with whom to bear pain and sorrow,
he is like a tree,
solitary on a hillside,
facing the buffeting winds alone.

(*Zaïre*)

One always dies for what has been a
reason for living.

(*Zaïre*)

When the festal tom-tom slows up,
it is to allow the guest to join the dance.

(*Zaïre*)

When bananas are turned
upwards, towards heaven,
they are one.
When they are turned
towards the earth,
their divisions appear.
It's like that with people too.

(*Madagascar*)

These proverbs belong to the history of Africa.
Those from Zaïre were chosen by Marie-Eugénie,
an ethnologist from Zaïre, who is presently
making a study of them.

WHERE CAN WE LOOK
FOR THE FESTIVAL IN INDIA?

CONSTANTINE (ALGERIA): *What can Moïz, a young Indian astrophysicist, who has lived almost all his life in contact with non-Christians, tell us about the preparation of the Council of Youth? He has been teaching for some time at the University of Constantine (Algeria) before leaving again for India.*

With Margarita and others, Moïz was a member of the Intercontinental Teams at Easter. Is it possible, in his view, to live the festival in India? What sense does this festival of liberation make in that country's situation? What is expected in India from the Council of Youth, and what can the youth of India bring to it?

In my country the monsoon has begun. With the first rain, hope is born again in the hearts of men. I remember the first rains of my childhood: that damp smell of burnt earth, eager for water; the children running in the streets and on the terraces, completely naked; that little song they sang:

> The rain has come!
> It came with the thunder,
> bringing us loaves, as hot as hot,
> and a stew of courgettes.

Since ancient times our poets and musicians have sung of the monsoon, that real springtime for India. The hope and the longing for it have remained in the hearts of men, bridging the centuries. And today in India we are walking towards an unknown future, preserving within us the singing and the music of the centuries, but bearing also the burden of the centuries.

I remember my first long stay in India, in 1970, after some time spent in Germany and France. I arrived straight from Taizé where the Council of Youth had just been announced.

Festival had been announced, and it was springtime. We had been singing of festival and of struggle. Festival and the monsoon, both are a hope in the hearts of men, and I was carrying within me the festival of all the nations. Everywhere men were rising up, ready to give much, even life itself, so that man shall be victim of man no more.

Where do we look for the festival in India? From the window of our flat I could see hovels. Below in the street filth, and men sleeping beside it. But sometimes, in the evening, someone would be singing, either in the street or else in a neighbouring house. The songs were hymns, several centuries old, hymns like psalms: 'My soul is athirst for thee, thou who art everywhere, thou who art in my heart, let me gaze on thy face'. Groups of people gathered round the singers, and perhaps for them, this was festival.

Last year along with the cell of four young men from Taizé, I visited a shanty-town in Bombay. For the social worker who accompanied us and for the old lady doctor who gave simple medical help three mornings a week in this shanty-town, festival was being among these people.

How many times had I passed this shanty-town; how many times had I turned my eyes away, pained and disturbed by that row of huts, built of anything that turned up: jute sacks, cartons, plastic bags, and a little corrugated iron for the luckiest ones. For the first time I was going right inside a shanty-town. I was with four young men from three countries in Europe: Robert, Rémi, Oliver, and Alberto. They had come to travel across India in order to understand and to share our cares and our hopes. Together we had realized that the words of the social worker were true: a shanty-town was much more repulsive from the outside than within. Inside we discovered a community much more united than many communities in the cities. There was the tomb of a Muslim saint whom they venerated, and the man responsible for the upkeep of the tomb was the 'Dada', responsible for the community. We introduced ourselves to him, and he went with us everywhere. We discovered that a spirit of mutual aid and also a political consciousness had developed. The family unit had remained intact and apparently all the children had homes.

In 1970 I worked for several months in a research laboratory in Bombay. This internationally famous laboratory represented another aspect of India: the India of factories, of industrial progress and of atomic centres. I was working with a small group of astro-physicists. Some of them had constructed in South India one of the most accurate radio-telescopes in the world.

The laboratory was the finest I had ever seen. The building, sober and functional, but vast, was surrounded by a magnificent garden with lawns sloping gently down to the sea. The entrance hall was a real exhibition of modern Indian painting and sculpture. Through these works of art yet another aspect of India could be perceived: an India searching for her identity, and certain of the works were like a cry of despair: 'Who am I? Is my soul in these ancient frescoes from the caves of Ajanta, or is it in this avant-garde painting?'

This despair and this quest for an authentic personality, I often found later among numerous young people, and others too, when I made a journey of more than 3000 km to explain the Council of Youth in India.

The first groups I went to were in Bombay itself: groups of students, and sometimes older people from Christian parishes. A year later the Taizé cell and I spoke in Bombay to groups of friends. High School pupils and older people. I realized, for the first time, how difficult it would be to prepare for the Council of Youth in India.

The Council was the response to a request by all the nations. Across the chaos and darkness of mankind, young and old were seeking one another and calling on each other to build a society of communion, a society where man would no longer be exploited. All these searchings had ended in the Joyful News announced in 1970 at Easter, but this news was also a starting point for the youth of all the countries. It meant preparing for the Council; that is to say, living the Joyful News, first oneself and also, and above all, with others.

How can we in India live out practically the Joyful News

which corresponds to the aspirations of all mankind? Set up communities for prayer? But Indians pray all the time and on all occasions. Far more than in the West, Indians pray constantly and at every moment of the day. Try to form groups of young people round a theme or common task? But the life of Indian youth is lived essentially within the family and besides, they have other concerns, employment above all. Be content to announce the Council and to urge young people to listen to each other and to unite? What would be the use, if there were no means of arousing life and dynamism to follow it up? What is the use of staying on the level of words?

What end do you start at to understand a country so vast, with such pronounced regional diversity? To be sure, twenty-three years of independence have profoundly changed the country, but no economic solution is yet in sight. There was the India of the hovels, the India of the peasants, the India of the industrialists and the scientists, and the India of the artists. Each face of India was looking in a different direction, and at first sight there was no common effort and no national feeling in the country. Everybody seemed to be working for himself, and while some were growing rich, the others were becoming poorer and poorer.

Wasn't it natural under these conditions for young men to become careerists and to think only of making a place for themselves in the sun? Wasn't it natural, too, for corruption to be everywhere present, and also political combines at every level, aimed at acquiring positions of power and influence?

Did the Council of Youth have its own word to say in this situation? Perhaps the only way of living the Joyful News in depth in India was to take part in the effort to develop the country. Cells of friends scattered throughout India, and always deeply involved in a concrete project for the liberation of man, could become catalysts to set off a process of awakening consciousness and of reconciliation. In these conditions the preparation for the Council in India would have to be discreet and long drawn out, with no great public meetings which would run counter to slow work in depth. More so than in other countries, the preparation of the Council in India would be an inner adventure, participating in the hidden, underground life of the Church. Perhaps, at the right moment, certain cells could meet to share together their experiences.

Viewing things in this way, little lights begin to shine for me in my country.

There is in South India, on the coast, a little village called Marianad. Assisted by friends of hers, Nalini, after years of work there, has succeeded in helping fishermen to organize themselves into a co-operative to break the power of the great fishing-boat owners. The project now also includes a school, a community centre, and a dispensary.

An Indian friend who studied in the United States and worked for years in Bombay in the same research laboratory as I did, left this laboratory to devote himself entirely to a project for rural education in Central India.

A girl I met last year in Bombay lived for two years in a hut among Untouchables who are being particularly exploited in South India. Taking advantage of their awakening political consciousness, already begun by the Communist Party and non-violent action groups, she took part, sometimes at the risk of her own life, in actions directed against the power of the landowners.

So there is no lack or concrete projects for the young Indians who want to organize themselves into Council of Youth cells—from work in cities to work in the country, the possibilities are numerous. Most of them will be projects for education, for the arousing of political and trade-union consciousness, and for community organization. Because of the static nature of social structures, peculiar to India, nothing leads us to believe that the present situation can be swiftly changed. All work in depth will be long and difficult.

In India we must never lose sight of the fact that the Christians are an infinitesimal minority among a great majority of Hindus and an important community of Muslims. For many young Christians the Church showed a triumphalist attitude during the colonial period and now her problem is to find an authentically Indian image. Side by side with the theological and liturgical renewal in which the philosophy and the sacred writings of the Hindus would be widely used, the Church must find her place in relation to a non-Christian society and define her social role. The Christians as a neutral group can become the driving force of a national reconciliation between Muslims and Hindus, two communities between which there are often riots and bloodshed, pretty well everywhere in India.

The Council is part of a great movement of men towards their own liberation. With hesitant steps, still in the dark, following a very small light, we are moving from death towards life.

Advancing towards
the Council of Youth

THIS IS
AN OPEN-ENDED BOOK

It remains open;
it has no conclusion.
You can't just say :
'I've understood!'
without beginning to move
towards the event itself.

Launched on an inner adventure,
we are staking out a public adventure.
When the time for the Council of Youth comes.
these two will remain,
the one treading in the footprints of the other,
with the ebb and flow of life itself.

The Council of Youth
will seek words and gestures
capable of revealing
a communion
in the sight of men.

Now to drop our masks,
widen the horizon of our vision,
to become men and women of communion :

led onwards,
by all who, before our time,
have followed Christ,
we are not the first to attempt
to make the faith that is in us
burst into life;
we are not alone
in our will for radical change
in the society of mankind;

reaching out
beyond the confines of our personal choices
we will struggle on,
eager for reconciliation;
not letting ourselves be held back
by rear-guard skirmishes;
not letting fragmentation
dislocate our communion,
nor unity reduce the pluralism,
but keeping ourselves open
to the universal;

making choices,
persevering to the end,
to the giving of our lives,
for the Church and for men;
a Church unshackled;
neither left nor right,
but ever ahead;
especially close to the man who is oppressed
and waiting to be freed;
we want to bring to birth
a life of communion
at whose heart struggle becomes festival.

But to prepare new births,
should we not return to the heart of the earth?
It is time to take to the catacombs.

And so,
as in the early Church,
in little groups,
Christians are meeting
in the darkness of the vaults.
But look, the funeral chamber
becomes a banqueting hall.
Songs rise in thanksgiving,
and the galleries carry the sound of the prayers

on and on into the chambers round
where we sense others are gathered.
As we descend into this underground movement
let us have no fear of being isolated :
for between us there is growing
a network of galleries
that frontiers cannot stop.

When one of us visited a community of young people
who know this world's hatred
for themselves and for their Church,
one of them said :
'Together, we have entered into commitments
on which we cannot go back,
for Christ is urging us on.'
On the Council of Youth, he added :
'It is like a peat fire
which ignites and spreads
some way below the surface,
it makes the ground swell up,
and suddenly
bursts out in an explosion.'

For us this is the time
of Holy Saturday :
Christ comes to inhabit our tombs,
and when the hour has come,
he will roll away the stone for us.

TEXTS BASIC TO THE PREPARATION FOR THE COUNCIL OF YOUTH

The 'Joyful News' and its origins
(Intercontinental Team, Easter 1970), p. 32-4

Threefold celebration of the Risen Christ, p. 38

The Risen Christ is going to prepare us to give our lives so that man be no longer victim of man
(Intercontinental Team, Easter 1971), p. 64

Imagination and courage to become signs of contradiction according to the Gospel
(Intercontinental Team, Easter 1972), p. 70

Struggle and contemplation to become men of communion
(Intercontinental Team, Easter 1973), p. 77

FOR NEWS OF THE PREPARATION OF THE COUNCIL OF YOUTH

The *Letter from Taizé* is published in eight languages, four times a year. Write to :
 Letter from Taizé
 F-71460 Taizé Communauté
 France.

DATE DUE

DEC 07 1995			